PIONEERS OF DAVIDSON COUNTY, TENNESSEE

Compiled by
EDYTHE RUCKER WHITLEY

CLEARFIELD

Reprinted for
Clearfield Company, Inc. by
Genealogical Publishing Co., Inc.
Baltimore, Maryland
1996, 1999, 2002

Originally published as part of the series
entitled *Tennessee Genealogical Records,*
Nashville, 1965
Reprinted: Genealogical Publishing Co., Inc.
Baltimore, 1979, 1981
© 1965 Edythe Rucker Whitley
© transferred to Genealogical Publishing Co., Inc.
Baltimore, Maryland 1979
All Rights Reserved
Library of Congress Catalogue Card Number 79-50041
International Standard Book Number 0-8063-0840-0
Made in the United States of America

PUBLISHER'S NOTICE

This work has been reproduced from the original
mimeographed edition. In spite of the blurred and
irregular image of the original, our printer has
made every effort to produce as sharp a reprint as possible.

CONTENTS

INTRODUCTION

In order for the researcher to understand the full
value of the records contained in this small volume, I
shall give a brief history of the settlement and formation
of Davidson County, Tennessee.

Early in the spring of 1779 preparations were made
at Watauga to plant a permanent settlement on the Cumberland.
The place selected was the bluff near the French Lick (now
Nashville). An account of the voyage can be found in
Clayton's HISTORY OF DAVIDSON COUNTY, published in 1880;
The first settlement is referred to in most any good history
of Middle Tennessee. These various publications relate some
of the events which were a part of the happenings along
their way.

Before reaching their destination the party was
split into two companies. Capt. James Robertson taking
command of one group while Colonel John Donelson became
the leader of the other group.

Colonel Donelson gave a list of those in his company;
A list considered most valuable to historians and genealogists.

After arriving at the spot we know as Fort Nashborough it was necessary for these settlers to set up some
kind of government. The result being "Articles of Agreement
or Compact of Government entered into by the Settlers on the
Cumberland River." This was 1 May 1780.   To this document
we find the names of persons who had arrived in the settlement at that time.

In 1784 the North Carolina General Assembly, granted
a petition to grant lands to those persons who had rendered
services in the settlement. This list again gives us a most
valuable piece of information.

We are indebted to Prof. W.W. Clayton, author of
HISTORY OF DAVIDSON COUNTY , 1880, for the 1787 tax list
showing the number of polls in each family.

This brings us to the names of persons registered
in Davidson County, Militia in 1812. So far as I am aware,
this list has never been published, and is one of very
great value. It contains almost every person in the county
who would have gone into the service under General Andrew
Jackson and engaged in the War of 1812. It also takes the
place of an 1810 census which was destroyed.

It was not until 1820 that we have a census available for the county. In fact Rutherford County,is the only

county which was saved of the 1,810 enumerations.

The Pension list of 1818 is our next most valuable item. I am including the list for West Tennessee, as Davidson County was at that time considered to be in West Tennessee. There is another reason for this also, many of those who were in Davidson County in 1800 and a few years later, had moved on westward. Some of them had been Revolutionary Soldiers, while others had served in the War of 1812, and some few possibly were in both.

The 1840 Davidson County, Census of Pensioners also is given herein, even though it has been published elsewhere.

It was in 1883 that we find the official pension list containing the names of service men or their widows at that time drawing Federal pensions. Of course, this is a most important list for their pension files in the National Archives contain a gold mine of history and genealogy.

I have included some other bits of information which I think will serve a purpose.

Originally there were three counties created in the Middle District, then called the "Mero" (Miro) District. These three counties were Davidson, Sumner and Tennessee. What is now Tennessee was previous to 1796 a part of North Carolina. Davidson County was created by an act of the Legislature of North Carolina, approved , October 6, 1783. It originally included most of the territory west of the Cumberland Mountains. Sumner County was carved and erected on November 17, 1786 by an Act of the North Carolina Legislature. In 1796 when Tennessee became a State it was necessary for the county of that name to relinquish the name. It was then that Old Tennessee County, was divided into two counties, bearing the names of Montgomery and Robertson.

Sumner County was divided in 1799 when a portion was made into Smith County, and at the same time another part of Sumner became Wilson County.

The Act creating Williamson County, cutting it from Davidson, was passed October 26, 1799.

On October 25, 1803 Davidson County gave up another large portion of her territory to form Rutherford County.

In 1807 Williamson was further divided and Maury County created. In 1803 Dickson County had been cut from Robertson and Montgomery, and in 1807 Hickman County was made from a part of Dickson. In the same year, 1807, Bedford County was formed from a part of Rutherford.

This gives the researcher a little better under-
standing of the location of the first settlers of the
Cumberland Settlement and the location of the pioneers in
the very early days, as well as draws a picture of their
pushing from the center in all directions.

This publication is especially valuable because of
the absence of a census for the first thirty five years of
Davidson County.It will suffice the loss of the 1810
census and goes far to bring the names of the pioneers up
to 1820 when a complete enumeration of the heads of families
of Davidson County, was made.

I have been a genealogist-historian for fifty years;
During which period of time I have accumulated a vast col-
lection on the people who came to the "Mero" District, many
of whom lie in unmarked graves; and, many others whose graves
once marked are no longer to be found on account of the fast
growing population and business expansion. There were those
who remained only a few years then moved on to other regions
westward and southwestward. Some fell by the way side and
their families moved on to clear the wilderness and establish
homes.

Among the names found in these various lists will be
many Revolutionary Soldiers , and Soldiers of the War of 1812,
therefore, it will be a contribution to these worthwhile
organizations and assist them in futhering their most
important work of preservation of American History.

Let's guard our sacred heritage by protecting and
preserving our County and State documents. Let us become
dedicated to the project of taking pride in our record
books and original documents.

Edythe Whitley

1604 South Observatory Drive
August 1965   Nashville, Tennessee 37215

COLONEL JOHN DONELSON'S COMPANY

The first immigration to the present site pf
Nashville --------- Col. John Donelson's Journal ----
Settlement at the Bluff ----------Built Fort Nashborough.
The names of the persons who came in this company are
given by Col. Donelson as follows:

John Donelson, Sr.	Benjamin Porter
Thomas Hutchings	Mrs. Henry (widow)
John Caffrey	John Cotton
John Donelson, Jr.	Thomas Henry
James Robertson's lady and children	Mr. Cockrell
	Frank Armstrong
Mrs. Purnell	Hugh Rogan
M. Rounsifer	Daniel Chambers
James Cain	Robert Cartwright
Isaac Neely	____ Stewart
John Montgomery	David Gwinn
Jonathan Jennings	John Boyd
Benjamin Belew	Reuben Harrison
Peter Looney	Frank Haney
Capt. John Blackemore	____ Maxwell
Moses Renfroe	John White
William Crutchfield	Solomon White
Mr. ____ Johns	____ Payne (killed)
Hugh Henry, Sr.	

Robertson County

Sumner County

BAKER STATION

Sycamore Cr

Mansker's Cr

Goodlettsville Cr

Dry Cr

JONES POND

Jones Island

Big Harpeth

MADISON

Neely's Bend

HERMITAGE

Ewing's Cr

Little Harpeth

Dry Cr

Cumberland River

Neely's Bend

Whites Creek

Davidson County

COCKRILL'S BEND

BURNS ISLAND

ROBERTSON ISLAND

RICHLAND

BELL'S BEND

Whites Bend

White's Creek

Nashville

DONELSON

Mc Crory

Bayou Cr

Gower's Ferry Buck Cr

BELLEMEADE

Sugar Tree

Brown's Cr

Mill Cr

Hamilton Cr

KINLEY'S

FLAT CR

BELVIEW

LITTLE HARPETH

County

OVERTON'S

Indian Cr

ANTIOCH

Mt. VIEW

Himbro

BRENTWOOD

Williamson

Rutherford County

Williamson County

Map of Davidson County,
shows some of the important places
and county lines, adjoining counties,
etc.

Signers "ARTICLES OF AGREEMENT OR COMPACT OF GOVERNMENT, ENTERED INTO BY THE SETTLERS ON THE CUMBERLAND RIVER, 1st MAY 1780."

Note: Civil Government was among the first needs of the settlers------ a voluntary compact was formed-------- Judges elected --------------- Articles of the agreement-------- List of signers---------- etc. It took all these and more to set up a form of Government.

Richard Henderson	William Gowan	John McMurty
Nathaniel Hart	John Wilfort	D'd Williams
William H. Moore	James Espey	John McAdams
Samuel Phariss	Michael Kimberlin	Samson Williams.
John Donelson, C.	John Cowan	Thomas Thompson
Gasper Mansker	Francis Hodge	Martin King
John Caffery	William Fleming	William Logan
John Blackemore,Sr.	James Leeper	John Alstead.
John Blackemore,Jr.	George Leeper	Nicholas Connrod
James Shaw	Daniel Mungle	Evin Evins
Samuel Deson	Patrick McCutchen	John Thomas
Samuel Martin	Samuel McCutchen	Joshua Thomas
James Buchanan	William Price	David Rounsavall
Solomon Turpin	Henry Kerbey	Isaac Rounsavall
Isaac Rentfro	Joseph Jackson	James Crooket
Robert Cartwright	Daniel Ragsdale	Andrew Crooket
Hugh Rogan	Michael Shaver	Russell Gower
Joseph Morton	Samuel Willson	John Shannon
William Woods	John Reid	Jonathan Drake
David Mitchell	Joseph Dpugherty	Benjamin Drake
David Shelton	Charles Cameron	John Drake
Spill Coleman	W.Russell Jr.	Mereday Rains
Samuel McMurray	Hugh Simpson	Richard Dodge
P.Henderson	Samuel Moore	James Grenn
Edward Bradloy	Joseph Denton	James Cooke
Edward Bradley, Jr.,	Arthur McAdoo	Daniel Johnston
James Bradley	Nathaniel Henderson	George Miner
Michael Stoner	John Evans	George Green
Joseph Mosely	Wm.Bailey Smith	William Moore
Henry Guthrie	Peter Luney	Jacob Cimberlin
Francis Armstrong	James Cain	Robert Dockerty
Robert Lucas	Daniel Johnson	John Crow
James Robertson	Daniel Jarrot	William Summers
George Freeland	Jesse Maxey	Lesois Frize (?)
John Tucker	Noah Hawthorn	Amb's Mauldin
Peter Catron	Charles McCartney	Morton Mauldin
Francis Catron	John Anderson	John Dunham
John Dunham	William McWhirter	Archelaus Allaway.
Isaac Johnson	Barnet Hainey	Samuel Hayes
Adam Kelar	Richard Sims	Isaac Johnson
Thomas Burgess	Titus Murray	Thomas Edmeston.

William Green
Moses Webb
Absalom Thompson
John McVay
James Thomson
Charles Thomson
Martin Hardin
Elijah Thomson
Andrew Thomson
William Seaton
Edward Thomelu
Isaac Drake
Jonathan Jennings
Zachariah Green
Andrew Lucas
    His
James X **Patrick**
    mark
Richard Gross
John Drake
John Holladay
Frederic Stump (in
    Dutch)
William Hood
John Boyd
Jacob Stump
Henry Hardin
Richard Stanton
Sampson Sawyer
John Hobson
Ralph Wilson
James Givens
James Harrod
James Buchanan,Sr.
William Geigch
Samuel Shalton
John Gibson
Robert Espey
George Espey

James Hamilton
Henry Dougherty
Zach. White
Burgess White
William Calley
James Ray
William Ray
Perley Grimes
Samuel White
Daniel Hogan
Thomas Hines
Robert Goodloe
Thomas W. Alston
William Barret
Thomas Shannon

James Moore

Samuel Moore
Elijah Moore
John Moore
Andrew Ewin
Ebenezer Titus
Mark Robertson
John Montgomery
Charles Campbell
William Overall
John Turner
Nathaniel Overall
Patrick Quigley
Josias Gamble
Samuel Newell
Joseph Read
David Maxwell
Thomas Jefriss
Joseph Dunnagin
John Phelps
Andrew Bushoney

Ezekiel Norris
William Farwell
William McMurray
John Cordey
Nicholas Framal
Haydon Wells
Daniel Ratleft
John Callaway
John Pleake
Willis Pope
Silas Harlan
James Lynn
    Thomas Cox
Hugh Leeper
Harmon Consellea

Humphrey Hogan

James Foster
William Morris
Nathaniel Bidlack
A.Tatom
William Hinson
Edmund Newton
Jonathan Green
    Edward Lucas
Philip Alston
John Phillips
    George Flynn
Daniel Jarrott
John Owens
James Freeland
Thomas Molloy
Isaac Lindsay
Isaac Bledsoe
Jacob Castleman
George Power
James Russell "

NORTH CAROLINA LAND GRANTS IN TENNESSEE 1784

North Carolina State and Colonial Records, Vol.
19, page 573, etc.

Monday 10 May 1784. The House-------------------
"Mr. Person from the Committee to which was referred
the Petition of the Inhabitants of Davidson County, Re-
ported as follows: vizt :- That the following persons, vizt -

John Cockrill
Ann Cockrill   formerly the widow Ann Johnston.
Robert Espy
John Buchannan
Cornelius Ruddle
James Mulkerin   (Mulherrin I am sure --- ERW)
James Todd
Isaac Johnston
John Gibson
Francis Amrstrong
John Kennedy Sen
Mark Robeson   (No doubt Mark Robertson ---ERW)
William Ellis
James Thompson
James Shaw
James Franklin
Henry Howdyshall
Pierce Castillo
Morris Shean   (Very likely Morris Shain or Shane --ERW)
William Logan
David Hodd   (Hood ?)
John White
Peter Looney
William Collins
Jonas Maniffee
Capt. Daniel Williams
John Evans
Andrew Thomson
Casper Mansoo   (Mansker, A Station named for him ---ERW)
George Freeland
Daniel Johnston
Edward Swanson
Andrew Kellow
Francis Hodge
John Mulkerin   (Mulherrin is the correct name----ERW)
James Freeland
John Tucker
James Foster
Amos Heaton   (Heaton's Station was one of the first --ERW)
Dennis Condry
Frederick Stump
Russell Gower

Andrew Ewin   (Very likely intended for Ewing ---ERW)
Thomas Prater
Isaac Lindsay
Moses Winters   (He settled in Robertson County,---ERW)
James Harris
John Browne
Lewis Crane
John Montgomery
Stephen Ray
Daniel Hogan
Thomas Spencer
Humphrey Hogan
Hayden Wells   (He became the land trader ---- ERW)
Henry Ramsey
John Barrow
Jno.Thomas
Wm.Streat
Saml Walker
David Rounsevall
Arthur MacAdoe
James McAdoe
Henry Turner
Saml Burton
John Dunham
Ephraim Pratt
James Robertson   (founder of Nashville ---- ERW)

each and every one of them, receive a grant of <u>six hundred and forty</u> acres of land, including their pre-emptions,
<u>without being</u> required to pay any price to the State for
the same, provided that every person receiving such grant
shall pay the office and surveyor's fees for the same.

        And the committee are further of opinion that
the Heirs or devisees of
Zachariah White
Alexander Buchanaam
James Leper   (The name found Leeper,Leiper,etc --ERW)
James Harrod
Alexander Thomson
David Maxwell
Robert Lucas
Timothy Tirrell
William Hood
Edward Carvin
William Nieley
James Shanklin
Samuel Morrow
George Kennedy
John Robertson
Abel Gowen, Sen   (Should be Gower --- ERW)
Abel Gowen Junr   (should be Gower ----ERW)

Nicholas Trammell
Philip Mason
James Turpin
Nathan Turpin
Jacob Stump
Nicholas Gentry
William Cooper
Jacob Jones
James Mayfield
William Green
William Johnston
Samuel Scott
George Aspie   (Very likely intended for Espie----ERW)
William Leighton
John Evans
John Crutchfield
Joseph Hay
John Searcey
Isaac Lucas
Patrick Quigley
Jacob Stull
Joseph Milligan
Abram Jones
David Fane
Benjamin Porter
Edward Larimore
William Gausney
Jonathan Jennings
David Gowin
Jesse Bialston
Joseph Renfrow
Philip Coonrod
William Gausney
John Bernard
John Lumsden
John Gilkey
Solomon Phelps
James John
Thomas Harney
Alexander Allerson
John Blackamore
James Fowler
John McMurtry   (Also spelled McMurtry, McMurtrey -ERW)
John Shockley
John Galloway
Isaac Lavavour   (possibly intended for Lavender---ERW))

who were killed in the settlement and defence of the said
County of Davidson, receive grants for the same number
of acres in the same manner, and on the same terms and
conditions as the former.

And as it appears that Christopher Gáis, Sen.,

Christopher Gais, Jun., Jonathan Gais, Kasper Booker,
Richard Breeze, Princis Cooke, Mark Nobles, John Kitts,
Isaac Mayfield, Samuel Hollis, Isaac Rounsvall, Enias
Thomas, Joshua Thomas, Caleb Winters, John Buchannan,
Sen., John Kennedy, Senr., John Kennedy, Jun., John
Castello, Robert Thomson and Swanson Williams,
part of them arrived from different places at the Cumb-
órlabd Settlements soon after the time prescribed by the
law for obtaining preemptions expired, and part of them
were there before the expiration of the time, but were
under age and, as it is also appears that all of them
have continued there ever since their arrival and assist-
ed in defending the Country, it is the opinion of the
Committee that they also receive free grants of the
same number of acres, as those mentioned above, and be
allowed the liberty of laying them wherever they can
find vacant lands and of entering them with the
entry officer, of Davidson County; on paying the usual
office fees--- All which is submitted

                    Thomas Person, Ch.

NOTE: See also N.C. Act. Vol. 24. p. 629, pertains
to the same action of the North Carolina General Assembly.

* * * * * * * * * *

NAMES OF PERSONS WHO WERE IN DAVIDSON COUNTY IN
1787, BEING THE FIRST YEAR IN WHICH. THE TAX ON LAND AND
POLLS WAS TAKEN, BEING (White) MALES OVER TWENTY-ONE YEARS
THREE HUNDRED AND SEVENTY TWO, AND BLACKS ONE HUNDRED AND
FIVE BETWEEN TWELVE AND SIXTY YEARS OLD.

(The figures indicate the taxable number in each
family).

Armstrong, William--------1	Cooper, James ----------1
Anderson, Henry-----------1	Crane, John-------------1
Allard, Hardy-------------1	Crawford,George --------1
Armstrong, Francis--------2	Carr,Robert ------------1
Bradshaw , H.-------------1	Contes, C --------------1
Boyles, H ----------------1	Cain, Jesse ----------- 1
Boyers, H ----------------1	Comstock, Thomas ----- 1
Berry,William------------1	Crutcher, Thomas-------1
Baker; Nicholas ----------1	Crutcher,William-------1
Baker, Reuben-------------1	Castleman, Jacob ------1
Baker; A-----------------1	Casselman,Andrew-------1
Borin, B------------------1	Clark,Lardner ---------1
Borin,John----------------1	Casselman, John -------1
Borin,William-------------1	Cox, Thomas ------------1
Boyd, James--------------1	Casselman, Benjamin ---1
Bell,Hugh----------------2	Cockrill, John---------1
Bushnell ,___-----------2	Cox, John --------------1
Baker, Joshua------------1	Cox, Phenix ------------1
Boyd, John---------------2	Carnahan, A ------------1
Bosley,James -----------17	Connor,William-------- 1
Bell, John---------------2	Canyer,William---------1
Brown, Thomas------------3	Cartwright,Robert -----5
Butcher, G.--------------1	Cochran,John---------- 1
Barrow, John-------------1	Craighead,Thomas B.----2
Brown,William -----------1	Donaldson, Jacob ------1
Blair, Thomas -----------1	Dunean,M ---------------1
Buchanan, Samuel --------1	Duncan,John-----------1
Byrnes, James -----------1	Delaney, James --------1
Buchanan,John------------1	Dodge,Richard ---------1
Bowan,Thomas-------------1	Duncan,William --------1
Bradford;Henry ----------2	Duncan,Samuel and John..2
Buchanan, Archibald------2	Donaldson,James -------1
Barnett, Robert----------1	Duncan, D -------------1
Blackemore, John---------8	Drake,Benjamin --------2
Blackamore, William -----2	Drake, John -----------1
Blackamore, Thomas-------2	Drake, Benjamin, Jr.---1
Blackamore,George -------1	Donaldson,William -----12
Boyd, Andrew ------------1	Donaldson, John--------3
Bodey,William -----------1	Dennings, Robert ------1
Boyd, John---------------1	Exheart, D.------------1
Cartwright, J.-----------1	Ewing, Andrew ---------1
Crow, D.-----------------1	Ewing, Alexander ------3
Coonrod, N.--------------3	Euman, E --------------1

Evan, Jesse -----------1
Edmonston, William,
    John, Robert, and
    Robert (2d)----------4
Evans, John -----------1
Espy,James -----------1
Elliot, Falkner -------1
Elliot, ___ -----------1
Frazer, John ----------1
Flancy, Daniel --------1
Ford,Isaac,Lewis,John--3
Freeland,Samuel -------1
Foster,James ----------1
Frazer,Daniel ---------2
French,Thomas ---------1
Gilliland, Hugh--------2
Guise, Charles and John-5
Gibson,John -----------1
Gramer, John---------- 1
Grant, Squire -------- 4
Gallaspy, William----- 1
Gentry,John-----------1
Geter, Argolas -----*-1
Glaves,Michael --------1
Guffy,Alexander and
    Henry---------- 2
Hogan,Daniel ----------1
Harrod; Bernard--------1
Hardin;M--------------1
Hooper; William -------1
Hooper,Absalom --------7
Hall, James ----------1
Handley,S ------------1
Huston;Ben------------1
Hardin, B-------------1
Hogan, H-------------1
Henry,Hugh and Isaac --2
Hay,David ------------3
Hodge, F-------------1
Harmand, Anthony ------1
Hampton, A.-----------3
Howard; John ---------1
Hollis, James, John,
    Joshua,Samuel --4
Heston, Robert and Amos.5
Hinds, William,Hamilton,
    James and Thomas--3
Harrold, Robert--------1
Hays, Robert ---------4
Hope, John------------1
Hannah, Jos ----------2
Hornberger, Phil ----1

Harris,James -----------1
Ilor, M ---------------1
Jones, James and John ----2
James, Daniel and Edward--2
James, Thomas----------7
Joslin,Ben------------1
Johns, Richard---------1
Johnston, William --------1
Kirkpatrick, John -------3
Kennedy,Robert----------1
Love, Joseph-----------1
Loggans,William --------1
Lewis, Thomas and Hugh ---2
Lenier, James and Henry --4
    Lucas,Andrew ----------1
Lyles, Hugh -----------1
Long,William ---------1
Lancaster, Jno.,2,and
    Wm.1.----------3
Lynn,Adam-------------1
Lindsay,James---------1
Luper, John-----------1
Martin, Joseph --------1
Marshall, William -------1
McAllister,James --------1
Mears, William ---------1
McNight,William---------1
McFarland, John---------1
Motheral; John----------1
Mitchell; William --------2
Mayfield;Isaac --------1
Marshall, John ---------1
McGowan,Samuel ---------1
McDowell, John ---------1
McNight, Robert --------1
Moore, William ---------1
Marlin ;Archibald -------1
McCarty,Jacob ---------1
McAntosh,Ben ----------1
Miller, Isaac ---------1
McAntosh,Thos, and Chas.--2
Murdoch,John----------1
Martin,Samuel ---------2
McCain, Thomas --------1
McFarland ,Thomas --------1
Maclin, William --------7
McGough, John ---------1
Molloy,Thomas, --------3
Miniss, Ben ----------1
Moore, Alexander -------1
McWhirter,William--------1
Martin,Archibald --------1

McCutchen, Patrick,
   Samuel and James--3
McSpadden ------------1
Murry, Thomas --------1
McLane, Ephraim--------1
McLane, Ephraim (2d)---1
McFadden,Jas.2, David
   1,----------------3
McFarlin,James----------2
MoSea, John-----------1
Nobles, Mark----------1
Neal, Thomas ----------1
Nash,William----------1
Nusam, Jonas ----------2
Neely,Isaac ----------2
Nevilles, George ------4
Owens, Charles and
   Arthur ----------2
Oglesby, John---------1
O'Neall, Jonathan ---- 2
Overall,Nathaniel
   and William ----2
Prince, Francis -------10
Phillips, John ----------1
Pennington,Jacob, ----4
Pittle, George --------1
Payne, Matthew, George
   and Josiah ----3
Peterson, Isaac -------1
Pollock,William B -----1
Pennington,Isaac ------3
Prochman,Phil---------1
Ruland, Lewis ---------1
Ray,Stephen-----------1
Rounsevall,David,Isaac,
   andJosiah---------3
Robertson, Alex,------2
Rpbertson,M and Mark --2
Ralston,Davis----------1
Ramsey,William --------1
Reckner, Coonrod ------1
Roberts, Isaac --------1
Reed, Alexander -------1
Robertson, Elijah------6
Robertson, Richard ----1
Robertson,James -------8
Ramsey,Josiah ---------2
Ross, James -----------1
Stuart,William --------1
Shaw,Joseph,William
   and James ------3
Shannon,Samuel,William
   and David------3

Shoat,Isaac ---------------1
Standley,David,Joseph and
   John ---------------3
Smothers, A.-------------1
Spiles, W.--------------1
Singleton-, St.John -------1
Smith,Jesse and Ezekiel ---2
Stump, Frederick ----------4
Stump,Frederick, Jr.-------1
Shannon,John --------------1
Steel,Andrew --------------1
Sutton, M.-----------------1
Stull, Zachariah ---------- 1
Scott, James --------------1
Swanson, Edward -----------1
Sides, P ------------------2
Shelby,Evan ---------------4
Thompson,Azariah ----------4
Thompson, Thomas, Laurence,
   and Andrew -----------3
Taylor,Thomas -------------1
Thomas, John,William,
   Isaac,and John -------4
Tillsforth, Isaac ---------3
Thompson,Charles, James
   and Robert ----------3
Taitt, William------------1
Titus, Ebenezer -----------1
Todd, James ---------------1
Tennin, H and James -----2
Walker, Samuel,John,Phil --3
Walker, John --------------2
Wells, H ------------------1
Winters, C and M.---------2
Wallace, Samuel -----------1
Willis, James -------------1
Williamson,James ----------3
Williams, Dan and Daniel---2
Williams, Sampson ---------1
Williams, William ---------2
Woolard, Isaac ------------1
White, Solomon ------------1
Wilcocks,Samuel -----------6

The following first appear as taxpayers: Hardiman, 1788; Hickman,1788; Hardins 1788; Charles Gordon 1789;Robert Weakley 1789; Jas. and David McGavock 1789; John Overton 1794; Andrew and John McNairy 1794; William Polk 1795;William Pillow 1795 and Gideon Pillow 1797.

TWENTY-TWO HUNDRED AND THIRTY FIVE FREE MALE INHABITANTS

IN DAVIDSON COUNTY, TENNESSEE, IN 1812.

Davidson County, Minute Book 1809-1812, page 826 etc.
Records of Davidson County Court of July Session 1812.
Enumeration of the Free Male Inhabitants of Davidson County,
Taken in the year 1812 a total of 2232 (2235).

No. Name.   No.   Name

In Captain Kincade's Company.
1. Nelson Whites
2. John Johnston, Jr
3. John Johnston, Senr.
4. Arthur Blair
5. John Lockhart
6. Hugh Lockhart
7. William Blakely
8. John McCain
9. Joseph Moore
10. Milton Gambrel
11. John Harper
12. Elisha Brewer
13. William Davidson
14. Adam Carper
15. Mordica Kelly
16. Robert Caldwell
17. Samuel Hayes
18 Isaac Johnston
19. Stephen Roach
20. Peter Eastley
21. Henry Guthrie
22. William H. Nance
23. John McFarland
24. Thomas Collins
25. Benjamin Barnes
26. Camdonr (?) McFaddin
27. Guy McFaddin
28. Michael Goodman
29. William Gibson
30. William Ogilvie
31. William Waldron
32. William Goodrich
33. Caleb Goodrich
34. Jesse Fly
35. John D. Fly
36. John M. Wright
37. Elias Peay
38. Isaiah Darrickson
39. Joseph Darrickson
40. Joseph E. Wilson
41. James Hailey

42. Miles Gibbs
43. John Strong
44. James Kincade
45. Aquilla Nod
46. Daniel Mitchell
47. Thomas Seawell
48. Benjamin Seawell
49. Jesse Morton
50. David Burton
51. Ephraim Thompson
52. Robert Thompson
53. Isaac Battle
54. Nathan Stancill
55. Hartwell Seat
56. Enoch Oliver
57. Samuel McKinney
58. Curtis Lemons
59. Linton Haile
60. Samuel Cross
61. James Goodwin
62. Samuel Thompson
63. John Morton
64. Isaac Scott a man of
           colour
65. William Lastly
66. James Lawrence
67. Lem Lawrence
68. James Laughlin
69. John Goodrich
70. Philip Wolf
71. George W. Wolf
72. Littleton Seats
73. William Harrace
74. Marcus Whitley
75. Hutchens Burton
76. Thomas Johnston
77. William Owens
78. John McCrory
79. John Stobach
80. Jordan Barnes
81. Joseph Watkins
82. James Hayes

83. Godfrey Dhelton
84. Elisha Brumfield
85. Jesse Johns
86. Thomas L.White
87. James Sanders

88. Elijah Owens
89. Jonathan Williams
90. River Jordan
91. Benijah Gray.

---------IN Captain Butler's Militia Company
92. Isaac Butler
93. John Frazer
94. James Mitchell
95. William Neely
96. William Trotter
97. Enis Walker
98. William Harris
99. Moses Frazer 100
100. John Pritchett   ?
101. Dennis S.Butler
102. William Blackamore
103. Nicholas Raymond
104. John Sanders
105. William Traser (?)
106. Smallwood Gaghill
107. Benjamin Cooper
108. Thomas Dickerson
109. Anthony Warwick
110. John Sale (or Cold ?)
111. Wilson Williams
112. David Craighead
113. Hugh Douglass
114. James Dennis
115. Nathaniel G.Childress
116. Thomas Scruggs
117. Walfield Scruggs
118. Henry Jackson
119. David Cartwright
120. Samuel Wray
121. William P.Robinson
122. Simon Williams
123. Edmond Goodrich
124. Richard Hankes
125. Anthony Hampton
126. Lemuel Herron
127. Robert Cartwright
128. Elisha Williams
129. Wyth Sims
130. Thomas A. Milville
131. Thomas Hudson, Senr.
132. William O Briant
133. Jacob Sumner
134. Robert Adams
135. Ingram Ralph
136. Robert Allen
137. James Frazer

138. Amos Nanny
139. Philip Hurt
140. Abner Hickson
141. Edmond Cornelius
142. John Henderson
143. James Cornelius
144. Meredith Johnston
145. Nathan Powell
146. Enoch Cunningham
147. John Dennis
148. Thomas Harney
149. Larkin Clay
150. Pilmore Coles
151. William Cole
152. Jacob Cartwright
153. John W. Cocke
154. Lewis White
155. Philip Walker
156. Matthew McCame
157. Thomas Folkes
158. John Monces
159. Samuel Neely
160. Willis Maclin
161. Matthew P.Walker
162. Ephraim Parham
163. Reuben Rucker
164. Wisnor Williams
165. William Hill.
166. Edward Sanders
167. John Beck
168. William Wray
169. Thomas B.Craighead
170. James Terrell
171. Jacob Dickinson Senr
172. Grosse Scrugg
173. John Walker
174. John Dew
175. Daniel Frazer
176. Ambrose Rucker
177. Edmond Rucker
178 Arthur White
179. Thomas Hudson Jr.
180. William Neely Junr
181. John A. Walker
182. Benton Pierce (?)
183. James Perry

184. Thomas Perry
185. Alexander Walker

186. Daniel Dennis
187. Elisha Herron

----- In Captain R.Boyd's Militia Company. ---

188. Francis Nusam
189. John Pew.
190. Richardson Phipps
191. Frederick Ivey
192. Thomas Crowder
193. Lewis Loyd
194. William Hubbs
195. John McGaugh
196. Francis Hardgreaves
197. Meshack Pinkston
198. John Forehand
199. James Pinkston
200. Wilkins Whitfield
201. Timothy Rieves
202. William Wren
203. Elijah Robertson
204. David Wren
205. James Rieves
206. Mason Fowler
207. Robert Simpson
208. Anderson Epperson

NOTE; Number 222 was not
used in the count. In a
few instances the paper
is so fragile that the
name has almost gone.
It is to be noticed that
the lists of various
companies almost show the
section of the county in
which they resided. Also
names which will later be
found in adjoining counties.
ERW

209. Thomas Parish
210. Robert Evans
211. Abner McGaugh
212. Archibald Walker
213. Aaron Franklin
214. Wm. Siozomore
215. Richard Boyd
216. Andrew Work
217. John Whitfield
218. Moses Night
219. Thomas DeMoss
220. Wm.Reaves
221. Elisha Garland
223. John Ivey
224. Thomas Loftin
225. Lewis DeMoss
226. James DeMoss Jr.
227. Duncan McCorthon ?(McCullom)
228. Peter Weaver
229. Jesse Woodard
230. Alexander Work
231. Leven Clark
232. Robert McGaugh
233. Philip Hart
234. Benjamin Stevenson
235. Stephen Hobbs
236. John Taylor
237. Israel Gabrick
238. William Charter
239. William Night
240. John Charter
241. Harrison Whitfield
242. James Demoss Junr
243. Alexander Patton
244. Matthew Patton
245. Eldridge Nusom
246. Henry Owens
247. Elisha Nicholson
248. Charles Hutton Senr
249. Samuel Hutton
250. Charles Hutton Junr.
251. John Barr
252. John Jones
253. Micajah McQuarry
254. William Gower
255. Jacob Hautt
256. John Myers
257. John Wilkes

258. Benjamin Wilkes	268. William Nusam
259. John Davis	269. Guy Smith
260. James Dufree	270. Benjamin Dunn
261. William Harwood	271. Lewis Dunn
262. Burwell Reaves	272. Philip Moody
263. Philip Cloyd	273. Josiah Horton
264. John Harwood	274. I (or J?) Granshaw
265. William Millar	275. John Smith
266. Sampson Millar	276. John Goodwin
267. Daniel Webb.	277. Isaac Greer

------In Captain Williamson's Company ----------------

278. Andrew Baldridge	317. John Hogan
279. Nathaniel Herbert	318. Francis Bladridge
280. James McCutchen	319. Floyd Hurt
281. William McCampbell	320. Cornelius Brewley (?)
282. Thomas Bell	321. Wm.B. Evans
283. Robert Bell	322. John Oliver
284. Nathaniel Bell	323. William Ragland
285. Joshua Owen	324. Payton Smith
286. William Newton	325. Edmond Reaves
287. Drury Clanton	326. William Bibb
288. Balam Hayes	327. John Rains Junr
289. Thomas Waller	328. Thomas Lightfoot
290. David Williams.	329. James Barnes Senr
291. Joel Barnes	330. Jesse Barnes
292. James Dixon	331. Absalom Davis
293. Robert Owens	332. John Grinder
294. James Turbeville	333. Samuel Philips
295. John Hughs	334. Samuel Fitzhugh
296. Willis Turbeville	335. William Grant
297. David Clanton	336. Robert C. Reaves
298. Eley Ewing	337. Harris Ogilvie
299. John Watson	338. Henry Plumer
300. Benjamin Seabourn	339. William Cherry
301. James Wright	340. Thomas Cotterall
302. Benjamin Turbeville	341. William Stoback
303. James Binfield	342. Pryor Cotterall
304. Adam Hope	343. Joseph N.Williamson
305. John Hope	344. Nelson Alfred
306. Thomas Hope	345. John McLean
307. George Linton	346. James McLean
308. James Bibb (Bell	347. Samuel Hope
or Belt ?)	348. John Bell
309. John Linton	349. George McClelland
310. Benjamin Turbeville	350. William W.Key
311. James Wright Junr	351. Robert Newton
312. James Wright Senr	352. Henry Robertson
313. Sterling Davis	353. Richard Clinton
314. John Davis	354. James P _____ (torn)
315. Charles Beasley	355. Wm.Ramsey
316. John Lynch	356. John Briley.

357. Samuel C.McNeese
358. James Nusam (?) (Torn)
359. George _____(torn)
360. Robert ____(torn)
361. Benjamin Riley
362. Samuel Bell, Esq.
363. David Watson
364. Adam Stobaugh
365. David Eakins
366. Robert Brown
367. Ezekiel Fitzhugh
368. David Bell
369. James Lych (Lynch ?)
370. Hugh Lynch
371. Jesse Pate
372. Nimrod Williams

373. Frederick Owen
374. Peter Owen
375. Frederick Owen Jr
376. Richard Williamson
377. Joseph Hollingsworth
378. William Ramsey Senr
379. John Haywood
380. Samuel Montgomery
381. James Leak
382. James Barnes Junr
383. James Sanders
384. Daniel Baldridge
385. Wm.Perkins
386. Nathaniel Wyche
387. John Stabauch
388. Wm.Thompson
389. Wm.Ham
390. S. Meredith
391. Bennett Blackmam
392. Isaac Currey

---------In Captain Haile's Militia Company ------

393. Robert Caldwell
394. Samuel Miles
395. Wm.Boyd
396. Wm.Hill
397. Robert Benningfield
398. George Hale
399. Enoch Gully
400. Peter Douge
401. Edward Tipton
402. Peter B.Stuart
403. Wm. Grimes , Senr
404. Wm.Grimes, Junr
405. John Demond
406. James Abel
407. Henry Dennis
408. Wm.Freeland
409. Samuel Dennis
410. James Freeland
411. John Duncan
412. George S. Allin
413. James Russell Senr
414. Enoch Douge.
415. Michael Specks.
416. Nathaniel Warren
417. Wm.Rosberry (Rasberry?)
418. Thomas Hooper
419. John Benningfield
420. Benjamin Pack,Sr.(Park)
421. Elisha Garland Junr
422. Jesse Garland

423. John McLovell
424. Jesse Kellam
425. Thomas Russell
426. James Russell Jr.
427. Wm. Russell
428. James Doran
429. Morning Doran
430. Custos Kellam
431. Jesse Hooper
432. Meshack Haile
433. Henry Levy
434. Nicholas Haile
435. John Campbell
436. James Lovel
437. Robert Lovell
438. Richard Champ
439. Goldsberry Champ
440. Micajah McQuerry
441. Elisha Nicholson
442. Jasper Aydolett
443. Jesse Woodward
444. John Barr
445. Kennedy Richardson
446. Charles Hutton Senr
447. Samuel Hutton
448. Charles Hutton Junr
449. Josiah Sugg
450. John Richardson
451. Leven Clark
452. Alexander Work

453. Charles B.Hutton
454. Joseph Neely
455. William Traviss
456. Benjamin D.Pook
457. Alexander W.McDaniel
458. Jesse Cox
459. Thomas Westbrook

460. Isaac Watkins
461. Wm. Watkins
462. Jesse Ward
463. Wm. Hughs
464. James Bonningfield.
465. Phillip Grimes
466. Joshua Sanders
467. James Baker
468. Wm.Levy
469. Wm.Champ

------In Captain Thomas's Militia Company ---------

470. Jesse W.Thomas
471. John Drury
472. Wm.McMurry
473. John Thomas
474. Anthony Clopton
475. James Love
476. John A.Allen
477. Sherrof Haile
478. Richard Smith
479. Zach Hayes
480. Benjamin Eaps ?
481. Thomas Tuckaway
482. Andrew Hays
483. Thomas Bernard
484. Wm. Murphey
485. Henry Hayes
486. Zach Neil (? torn)
487. Andrew Edmondson (torn)
488. Leonard Keeling
489. Henry ____(torn)
490. Edward____(torn)
491. Samuel Blair (torn)
492. Charles Mulherrin
493. Wm.Birthright
494. James Lee
495. Greaves Pennington
496. Wm.E. Carter
497. James McBride
498. Robert Wood
499. John S.Butler
500. Richard Compton
501. John Buchanan (Whitehead)
502. Archibald Pullin
503. John Napier
504. John Roberts
505. Allen McNeese
506. Hull McNeese
507. James Samples
508. Ancylin Burns

509. James Carter
510. John Carter
511. Samuel McMurry
512. Joshua Tuckaway
513. Peter Tuckeway
514. Daniel Tradewell
515. Wm.Quarles
516. Zach Harrison
517. Richard Neliday (?Holiday)
518. Silas Flournoy
519. Seth Cason
520. James McFerrin
521. John McFerrin
522. Edmond Owen Junr
523. Henry Owen
524. Thomas Camp
525. John Tindal
526. John C.Hall
527. John B.W Hall
528. Archibald Hall
529. Drury M. Allen
530. Jesse Carroll
531. Tarlton East
532. James Austin
533. Shedrack Bryant
534. James Carter, Senr.
535. George W. Chalton
536. John Sheppard
537. Wm. Bibb
538. James Exum
539. Wm.Hall
540. Samuel Scott
541. Michael Snyder
542. Samuel Allen
543. Henry White
544. Jeremiah Grizzard
545. John Edmondson Senr.
546. David Buchannan
547. George Keeling.

548. John Greaves
549. John Blair
550. John Hoggatt
551. Edmond Cooper
552. Abraham Sandifer
553. James Priestly
554. John Buchanan
555. John Moneese
556. Robert Samples
557. John Carter, Senr
558. John Camp
559. Wm. Cannon
560. Charles McHall
561. James Buchanan
562. Edmond Owens, Senr.

563. Wm.Matlock
564. James Mulherrin
565. Camelia John ?
566. John Erwin
567. Nathaniel Brown
568. Samuel Williams
569. George Barnard
570. Jeremiah Roberts
571. Robert Sample Junr
572. Robert Edmondson Junr
573. Joseph Cassellman
574. John Goodrich

---------In Captain Mullen's Militia Company -----

575. Robert Rasberry
576. Francis Hodge
577. James Hodge
578. George Hodge
579. Jasoph McBride
580. Wm.Sneed
581. Benjamin Cassellman
582. Wm.Emethon (?)
583. John Dillahunty
584. George West
585. Wm.Mullen
586. Hoorge Beeton
587. Asa Beeton
588. Joel Anderson
589. John Boyd
590 Robert Boyd
591. Wm.Betts
592. Jonathan Betts
593. Richard Compton
594. Wm.Compton
595. Robert Thomas
596. Andrew Connelly
597. Peter Connelly
598. Peter Caffrey
599. Ezekiel Inman
600. Robert Page
601. James Gillam
602. Benjamin Greer
603. Martin Greer
604. John C. Bradshaw
605. Henry Kirkpatrick
606. Alexander Craige
607. Jacob Thompson
608. Robert Thompson

609. James Donnelly
610. John Donnelly
611. Francis Hargrove
612. David Singletary
613. John Singletary
614. John Johns
615. Daniel Dunham
616. John Harding
617. Wm. Griffin
618. Elias Waits
619. Wm.Davis
620. Edmond Smith
621. James Maxwell
622. Wm.Montgomery
623. John Bowles
624. Abraham Cassellman Junr
625. John Dunham
626. John Shute
627. Black David
628. Howel Tatum
629. George Elmore
630. Nathan Williams
631. James Williams
632. John Johnston
633. Edmond Williams
634. Harris Cobler(or Cabler)
635. John Nichols
636. Solomon Holder
637. John Goodman
638. Wm.Bumpass
639. James Davis
640. Hensley Cobler Senr.(Cabler ?)
641. Hensley Cobler Junr (Cabler ?)
642. Thompson Ozburn.

643. Robert Lazenby
644. Alexander Lazenby
645. Wm.Armstrong
646. Johnston Vaun ? (Vann)
647. Joseph Erwin
648. Wm.Howlett
649. Wm.Shelton
650. Henry Compton
651. Wm.Compton Senr
652. John Barker Junr.

653. Wilson Barker
654. Laban Barker
655. John Barker
656. Robert Williams
657. Samuel Jasman (Inman?)
658. Joshua Dycus
659. Richard Kingston.
660. Thomas Emerton
661. Augustus Kerney

-----In Captain Barnhart's Militia Company -----------

662. Robert C.Foster
663. Wm.Dickson
664. John Williams
665. Nathaniel Ashley
666. Clement Hall
667. Thomas Addair
668. George Ridley
669. John Ray
670. John Childs
671. John Cobler (Calber ?)
672. Saml Ham
673. James Meneese
674. Wm.Neal
675. Joseph Green
676. Aquilla Carmick
677. Walter Kibble (Keeble ?)
678. Thomas Oden
679. Thomas Wilcox
680. Wm.Bryant
681. Wm. Parham
682. David Cummins
683. John Blair
684. Henry Cromer
685. Jonathan Hagan
686. John Topp
687. Wm.T.Lewis
688. Jonas Maniffee Senr
689. Jonas Maniffee Junr
690. Thomas Maniffee
691. Francis Cobler (?Cabler)
692. Wm.Rains
693. Thomas Everitt
694. John Everitt
695. Laban Estes
696. Stephen Hord
697. Jeptha Stephens
698. Austin M.Wade
699. Wm.Wharton
700. John Waugh
701. George Brown.

702. Henry Phoenix
703. John Moore
704. Jesse Cutter
705. Thomas Hopper
706. Littleton Perry.
707. Joseph Hopper
708. James Hopper
709. John Garrett
710. John Corbitt
711. Daniel W. Taylor
712. David Hays
713. Wm.Hays
714. Thomas Thompson
715. Benjamin P.Parsons
716. Lawrence Thompson
717. Thomas Harlow
718. Sampson Linley ?
719. Wm.Marks
720. Sampson Edwards
721. James Whittsit
722. Richard Hubbard
723. John Rains Senr
724. Joel Lewis
725. Richard Kingston
726. Joseph Vick
727. Wm.Roberts
728. Hensley Handy
729. John Barrhart
730. Thomas Thornburgh
731. Wm.Osmar (?Asmer)
732. Jason Thompson
733. Michael C.Dumos ?
734. Michael Campbell
735. George M. Deadrick
736. Thomas Thompson Senr
737. Frederick Hopper
738. James Porterfield
739. Tob. Horn
740. Solomon Williams
741. Thomas Crantz

742. John Crants   744. Llad ? Metcalf.
743. Henry Soliss ?

------------In Captain Cloyd's Militia Company -------

745. Samuel Shannon
746. Pitt Woodard
747. Daniel Woodard
748. Edward Woowoad
749. Norrid (or Novil)
  Calthrop
750. Clayton Calthrop
751. David Cloyd
752. David Balintine
753. James Marshall.
754. John Cleaves (?Gleaves)
755. John Lucas
756. Jeffrey Johnston
757. Moses Fowler
758. Barnabas Bayler (?Boyles)
759. John Bayler (?Boyles)
760. George Taylor
761. Francis Taylor
762. Samuel Taylor
763. Newsom Harris
764. Martin Fryer
765. John Holmes
766. Abijah Holmes
767. Alexander Reed
768. David Ralston
769. John Ralston
770. George Ralston
771. John Motheral
772. James Motheral
773. John Gilbert
774. Wm.Edens
775. Absalom Hooper Jr.
776. David Walker
777. John McCaslin, Senr
778. John McCaslin, Junr
779. Aquilla Jones
780. Thomas Shivers
781. Robert Holt
782. William James
783. William Shaw
784. Absalom Hooper Senr
785. Nimrod Hooper
786. James Gill
787. Drury Scruggs
788. Theophilus Scruggs
789. Langhorn Scruggs
790. James Moses

791. John Iredak Senr.
792. Samuel Morris
793. Lomuel Morris
794. Thomas Morris
795. George Wharton
796. Samuel E. (or L) Wharton
797. James McAlister
798. Douglass Puckett
799. David Hunter
800. Jacob Dickinson
801. Joseph Philips
802. Etheldred Horn
803. Nathan Barnes
804. Matthew Horn.
805. Wm.McCaslin
806. John McCaslin Jur.
807. Joseph Motherill
808. Isaac Newlin
809. Joel Beavers
810. Thomas Cold
811. Matthew Jackson
812. James Emerson
813. John Fowler
814. Elisha Bellamy
815. Britain Harper
816. Richard C. Phelin
817. Joseph Look
818. Daniel Fowler
819. Wm.Holt
820. John B. Dilyard
821. Wm.Cathrop
822. Ruben Noel
823. Asa Morton
824. Jacob Morton
825. Wayfield Scruggs
826. Enoch Cunningham
827. Lowry McDaniel.

-------IN NASHVILLE AND IT'S VICINITY.-------------

828. Wm.H.Bedford	877. John Baird
829. Isaac Sittler	878. Robert Searcy
830. Anthony Foster	879. James W.Sittler
831. John Dickinson	880. Lemuel T.Turner
832. Wilkins Tannyhill	881. John Frazier
833. Robert Smily	882. Josiah Nichols
834. John Price	883. Jenkins Whiteside
835. John R. Bedford	884. Boyd McNairy
836. Felix Robertson	885. Andrew Ewing
837. McNairy Robertson	886. Henry Ewing
838. Thomas Yeatman	887. Wm.Lytle
839. James Weatherall	888. Thomas Claiborne
840. Thomas Masterson	889. Alexander Porter
841. James Candon (or Cardon)	890. John Allen urter
842. George Payzer	891. Banay Higgins
843. John Anderson	892. John Young
844. John Deathridge	893. Thomas Williams
845. Thomas Deathridge	894. George Garrett
846. Thomas Kirkman Senr	895. Lodowick George
847. David Cummins	896 _____ Yeatman
848. Robert Martin	897. Robert McQuillam
849. Henry Stobaugh	898. Albert Osborn
850. Turner Shaw	899. Daniel McIntosh
851. Wm.Eastin.	900. Andrew Mitchell
852. Andrew Haynes	901. Thomas Garret.
853. John Sommerville	902. Thomas Cary
854. Samuel Elam	903. Moses Baits
855. Charles Cassady	904. John Ambison
856. Thomas Hill	905. John Gibson
857. Joseph Park	906. Andrew Cammeron
858. Francis May	907. Thomas Brenson ?
859. Thomas Deadrick	908. Foster Sayers
860. David Deadrick	909. James Jackson
861. Rondal McGavock	910. James Hanna
862. John L.Ewing	911. Alexander Richardson
863. Jacob McGavock	912. Thomas Shackleford
864. John C. McLamore	913. Jeptha Mosley
865. James Vaulx	914. John Zigler
866. Thomas Childress	915. Martin Rice (?Rue)
867. Thomas H.Fletcher	916. John Hancock
868. Charles Hickerson (or Dickerson ?)	917. Matthew Clopton
869. Edward Raworth	918. Robert Armstrong
870. John Hiter	919. Wm.Allen
871. John Jackson	920. Robert Price
872. Robert McFarland	921. Cornelius Vanbuskirk
873. Elizha S. Hall	922. John Nichol
874. Joseph Inglman	923. Isaac Skiller
875. Nathaniel Peck	924. James Porter
876. James Camp.	925. Joseph Porter
	926. Ephraim Pritchett.

927. George Morgan
928. Wm.Morgan
929. Richard Tyree
930. Elisha Dickerson
931. Peter Myers
932. Jacob Horns
933. Thomas Patton
934. John H.Smith
935. George Martin
936. Stephen Cantrill
937. Thomas I (or J) Read
938. Joshua Pilcher
939. John B. Seawell
940. Mark R. Rentfro
941. Joseph Bronison
942. Wm.Patton
943. Paul Kingston
944. John Wilson
945. George Hewlett
946. Ulsey G.Mimo (or Mims)
947. Wm.Seay
948. Samuel Seay
949. Thomas Ramsey
950. Henry Wyand ?
951. Benjamin I (J?) Bradford.
952. Henry Doughty
953. Daniel Bryson (Brysor)
954. Robert Rentfro
955. Joseph Woods
956. Wm.W.Drake
957. Joshua Nevills
958. Duncan Robertson
959. Thomas Porter
960. John P.Smith
961. Jacob Sumner
962. John Priest
963. Wm.Dew
964. Timothy Demumbreum Senr
965. Timothy Demumbreum Junr
966. Joseph T. Elliston
967. James Connelly
968. David Moore
969. Thomas G.Bradford
970. John G.Berry
971. Wm.Iredall
972. Wm.Wallace
973. Augustus Wilkerson
974. Joseph Wallace
975. Moses Wallace
976. James Buck
977. Ernest Benoit
978. Henry Gross

979. David C.Snow
980. Isaac Davis
981. James Irwin
982. Thomas Kirkman Junr
983. Archibald Scott
984. Robert Scott
985. Wm.Owen
986. Samuel Frazer
987. Richard Napier
988. Joseph Coleman
989. Bosley (?Torn) H.Meanly
990. (torn) Roper
991. James P. Downs
992. Wm.Richard
993. Eli Talbott
994. George Perkins
995. John Falwell
996. Moses Eakins
997. Andrew D.Scott
998. Matthew Moore
999. Peter Dickey
1000. Thomas Eastin
1001. John Givins
1002. Robert B.Curry
1003. Josiah Curry
1004. Frederick Fisher
1005. Cais Williams
1006. James Milton
1007. Elihu Marshall
1008. Wm.Lintz
1009. Wm.G. Probart
1010. Bernard P. Keman ?
1011. Samuel Stout
1012. Fleming Ward
1013. John Bettis
1014. Wm·Cropper
1015. Joseph Ward
1016. Isaac Paxton
1017. Eldridge Green
1018. James G.Hicks
1019. Etheldred Williams
1020. Samuel Anderson
1021. Samuel Richard
1022. Charles McCarnahan
1023. Edward D.Hobbs
1024. Collins S.Hobbs
1025. Philip Watkins
1026. Archibald Geary
1027. George Maxey
1028. Young Davis
1029. Aaron Day
1030. Solomon Burns

1031. Edward Walker	1084. Banister Hatchett
1032. Thomas Hankins	1085. Leonard Parker
1033. Wm.Watkins	1086. James Gray
1034. James Bradbury	1087. Bennet Searcy
1035. Leonard Porcher	1088. John Tandsherd
1036. John T.Bell	1089. Wm.Connelly
1037. James Crivohloe	1090. Wm.Rutherford
1038. Thomas Hankins	1091. Clayton Talbott
1039. James Crutcher	1092. Wm.L. Boyd
1040. Archibald Dewalt (Dewall)	1093. Levy Claybrook
1041. Henry Cooper	1094. Richard D. Wall
1042. Daniel White	1095. Samuel Manning
1043. Lester Morris	1096. Samuel Goode
1044. James Williams	1097. John Pence
1045. Wm.McCay	1098. Archy Geary
1046. George Bell	1099. Thomas Hrady
1047. W.Bosworth	1100. Wm.Kent
1048. Collins Bosworth	1101. Allen Richardson.
1049.Robert Stainback	1102. Daniel McBeam
1050. Wm.Smith	1103. John McCaffrey
1051. Thomas Williamson.	1104. Wm·Slone (or Stone)
1052. John S.Williamson	1105. James Benning
1053. Ellis Maddox	1106. Philip Thomas
1054. Thomas Mosley	1107. Christopher Chaistian
1055. Moses T. Brooks	1108. David Irwin
1056. Robert Stothart	1109. Ceasar Prince
1057. Cliver B.Hayes	1110. Wm.P. Anderson
1058 John Newman	1111. Charles B. Neilson
1059. James Roan	1112. Jonathan Magnus (Magness)
1060. Anthony Foster, Junr	1113. Benjamin White Junr
1061. Washington L.Hanum	1114. David Magnus (Magnees)
1062. Felix Grundy	
1063. Joshua Haskell	
1064. Charles Marton	
1065. Lemuel P. Montgomery	
1066. Thomas Crutcher	
1067. Littleton Johnston	
1068. Thomas Willett	
1069. David McGavock	
1070. James McGavock	
1071. John McGavock	
1072. Patrick Bigley	
1073. Alpha Kingsley	
1074. Wm.Carrol	
1075. David Isdald	
1076. Ezekiel Squires	
1077. Jonas Ahard ?	
1078. John B.Gawthmey	
1079. W.Blacfare	
1080. Wm.Wood	
1081. Wm.Taitt	
1082. Nicholas B. Pryor	
1083. David Hayes	

-------In Captain Henry's Militia Company ----------

1115. Wm.Henry	1165. Daniel Jones
1116. Wm.Allon Senr	1166. John Jones
1117. Wm.Allen Junr	1167. Samuel Smith
1118. Hardy Mitchell	1168. Wm.Byers
1119. Thomas Jackson	1169. Henry Cowden
1120. Dempsey Sawyers	1170. John Jackson
1121. Henry Brown	1171. Vincent Cartwright
1122. Mason Richardson	1172. Samuel Sawyers
1123. Samuel Carroll.	1173. Newton Edney
1124. Jarvis James, Junr	1174. Wm.Nusom
1125. Alson Linton	1175. Daniel Richardson
1126. James Conner	1176. George Greer
1127. James Demoss	1177. Berry Greer
1128. Richard Hart	1178. John Goodwin
1129. Robert Shannon	1179. Henry Brown
1130. Lauzuras Inman	1180. Robert Kennedy
1131. Elisha Roads	1181. Hugh Allison
1132. Abraham Taylor	1182. Matthew Tennison
1133. James Marlan	1183. Samuel Tennison
1134. James Allison	1184. Wm.McCollum
1135. Henry Bryan	1185. Samuel Bryan
1136. John Davy	1186. Wm.Henry
1137. John Harding	1187. Levin Edney
1138. Nat. Gillam	1188. Wm.Grier (Greer ?)
1139. Isaac Greer	1189. Newell Gracey
1140. Silas Dillahunty	1190. Zachary Allen
1141. Joseph Davy	1191. James Conner
1142. Richard Davy	1192. Thomas Allen
1143. James Koonce	1193. John Marlin Senr
1144. George Kponce	1194. James Marlin
1145. Benjamin Pritohett	1195. James Griffin
1146. Levi McCallum	1196. Wm.Dillahunty
1147. Wm.Roach	1197. Elisha Spence.
1148. Isaac Jones.	1198. Seth Davis
1149. Bartholomew Stephens	1199. John Strean ?
1150. Andrew Boyd	1200. Samuel Mays
1151. Timothy Jones	1201. Benjamin Pritchett
1152. Wm.Ellis	1202. Wm. Ba_____?
1153. Wm.Brannon	1203. Thomas Gillum
1154. Thomas Williams	1204. Robert McLin
1155. John Gracy	1205. Bryant Boon
1156. Lemuel Jones	1206. Wm.Tho Shelton
1157. David Givens (? Gwin)	1207. Wm.Ellis
1158. James Kinsey	1208. John H.David
1159. Isaac Little	1209. Wm.Winston
1160. Samuel Sawyers	1210. Samuel Winston
1161. John Allen	1211. Ranchey McDaniel
1162. Wm.Bryan	1212. Thomas Westbrook
1163. John Cartwight	1213. Wm.Helborne
1164. Allen Forehand	1214. John Kennedy

1214. **Robert Kennedy, Senr**
1215. John Orton
1216. Leodowick Williams
1217. Lewis Demoss
1218. John Martin
1219. Edick Councill
1220. Isaac Blount
1221. C.

1221 **Samuel Orton**
1222. Wm.Latham
1223. Abraham Cassellman.

NOTE: Original list had 2 numbered 1212, picked up
at 1214. ERW.

-----------In the Company formerly Liles Company.-----

1224. Wm.R.Bell
1225. Henry Lile
1226. Philip Shute
1227. George Haggerty
1228. Richard Kingston
1229. James Davis
1230. Jonathan F.Robertson
1231. Jarvis Scales
1232. Wm.Scales
1233. Anthony Scales
1234. Joseph Horton
1235. James H.Williams
1236. Nathan Williams
1237. John Johnston
1238. Caleb Hewitt
1239. John D. Simington
(? Livingston)
1240. Wm.Tally
1241. Drury Jordan Senr
1242. Drury Jordan Junr
1243. John Seavy (maybe
Searcy)
1244. Wm.B. Robertson.
1245. John Williams
1246. Washington Curtis
1247. James Robertson
1248. Elisha Williams
1249. James Watson
1250. Hugh F.Bell.

1251. Solomon Clark
1252. Beal Bosley
1253. Wm.Bell
1254. Benjamin Phillips
1255. Zachariah Waters
1256. Mathew Barrow
1257. Archibald Walker
1258. Wm.Powell
1259. Philip A. Ripsumer
1260. Robert Hewitt
1261. Jackson Harville
1262. Isaac Chandler
1263. Wm.Chandler
1264. Minajah Creel
1265. John Williamson
1266. Robert Cunagin
1267. James Allen
1268. Wm.Allen
1269. Phillip Matthis.
1270. Willia Stringfellow
1271. Henry Crutchlow (Critchlow ?))
1272. Joshua Mullen
1273. John Newell
1274. Mark Newell
1275. John Connelly
1276. John B. Craighead
1277. Abner McGaughey
1278. Samuel Newel.

---------In Dempsey Morris Company --------------------

1279. Wm.Curtis
1280. Wm.Hickman
1281. Abraham Noblett
1282. Thomas Hickman
1283. Harris Dowlin
1284. Shadrack Jones
1285. Ira Pierce
1286. John Pierce
1287. Jesse Pierce
1288. Thomas Pierce.

1289. Ezekiel Smith
1290. Stewart Famborough
1291. George Waters
1292. James Reaves
1293. Daniel Reaves
1294. Elijha Reaves
1295. Elisha Reaves
1296. Wm.Coon
1297. Hisia Chissine (Shissm)
1298. Thompson Simpkins Junr

28

1299. Joseph Simpkins	1330. Thomas Gilbert
1300. Joshua Sykes	1331. Wm.Hunt (Hust ?)
1301. Wm.Walker	1332. Elijah Hunt (Hust?)
1302. Samuel Lenox (Lennox)	1333. Wm.Waters
1303. Cordy C.Peebles	1334. Enoch Kennedy
1304. Jesse Ellis	1335. Robert Heaton
1305. Benjamin Hyde	1336. Thomas Heaton
1306. James Martin	1337. John Drake Senr
1307. Isaac Mayfield	1338. John Drake
1308. Isaac Kennedy	1339. Willie Dawson
1309. Jnoathan Drake	1340. Jessee Everitt
1310. Jacob Cagle	1341. Edmond Hyde
1311. Michael Waggonner	1342. Laban Abernathy
1312. Michael Vincent	1343. John W. Edney ((Blotted)
1313. Joseph Rusk (Rush ?)	1344. Wm. Gower
1314. Lewis Williams	1345. Samuel Haw
1315. Dempsey Morris	1346. Asa Pace
1316. Micajah Morris	1347. Samuel Smith
1317. John Criddle	1348. Peter Harrington
1318. Thomas Watts	1349. Nathan Bennett
1319. Daniel Ross.	1350. John J. Nicholson
1321. Wm.Turner	1351. James Lusk
1322. Jesse Smith	1352. Wm.Mitchell
1323 Thomas Parker	1353. Wm. Nelins (?) (Nelms ?)
1324. Meredith Jordan	1354. Benjamin Jordan
1325. James Everett	1355. Wm.Roland
1326. Simon Everett	1356. Balaam Roland
1327. James Fox.	1357. Jordan Roland
1328. Wm.Gilbert	1358. Thomas Smith
1329. Nelson Loisny (Lowry ?)	1359. William V. Jordan
	1360. Terrell Sykes
NOTE: No.1320 was omitted	1361. John Lugert
in the original. ERW	1362 Joseph Wootson (Watson ?)
	1363. Henry Lacy

----------- In Capt. Creel's Militia Company -----------

1364. Robert Butler	1380. Wm.C.Wood
1365. Richard Taitt	1381. Joseph Cassellman
1366. Philip Wilson	1382. David Cassellman
1367. Allen Dodson	1383. Henry Cassellman
1368. John Dowlen	1384. Benjamin Cassellman
1369. Samuel Brown	1385. Ali Cherry
1370. William Wilson	1386. Timorhy Dodson
1371. Hugh Hays	1387. Joseph Cooke
1372. Moses Earhart	1388. John Briant
1373. Elijah Dodson	1389. Flowers Migigor (McGregor ?)
1374. Joseph Shores	1390. John Pannell
1375. Frederick Pinksley	1391. Charles Wright Junr
1376. Henry T.Rucker	1392. Holess Wright
1377. Joseph Newman Jr.	1393. Charles Wright Sner
1378. Harner Sanders	1394. William Wilson.
1379. John H.Camp.	1395. Wm.Creel

1396. John Napier	1429. Michael Glaves
1397. John Shaw	1430. Philip Earhart
1398. Seven Donelson	1431. Robert Earhart
1399. Cleman M. Donelson	1432. Jacob Earhart
1400 John Ward	1433. Robert Hayes
1401. Severn Donelson	1434. Severn Donelson
1402. Joseph Holt	1435. John Sanders
1403. Elsha Maddon (Maddox?)	1436. John Shaw
1404. John Taitt	1437. Moses Strain
1405. Zedekiah Taitt	1438. John Donelson Junr
1406. Jacob Earhart	1439. John Donelson Senr
1407. Thomas Molom ?	1440. Alexander Donelson Jun
1408. John Cassellman,Junr	1441. Samuel Donelson
1409. Absalom Gleaves	1442. Alexander Donelson Senr
1410. John Cassellman, Senr	1443. John Bosley
1411. James Humphries	1444. James R.Bosley
1412. Thomas Bradshaw	1445. Francis Sanders
1413. John McNeal	1446. Franklin Sanders
1414. Thomas Gleaves	1447. Richard H. Jones
1415. Campbell Hayes	1448. Edward Bounderant
1416. Wm.Stuart	1449. Arthur Owens
1417. Robert Mann (Monn)	1450. Burwell Owens
1418. George Hogan (Hagan?)	1451. Wm.Brooks
1419. Elmore Melvin	1452. Andrew Jackson
1420. Wm. Melvin	1453. Thomas Overton.
1421. Samuel Scott	1454. John Fields
1422. Josiah Cunningham	1455. Richard Booker
1423. Henry Cowgill	1456. Edward Ward
1424. John Cowgill	1457. Wm.Sanders
1425. Wm.Newsum	1458. Benjamin Mitchel
1426. Abner Cowgill	1459. Thomas Watson
1427. Wm.Taitt	1460. John Smith
1428. James Jamison	1461. John Brown

--------In Captain Birdwell's Militia Company ------

1462. James Rice	1478. Wm. Criddock
1463. James Yarbrough	1479. Thomas Showers
1464. Wm.Caldwell, Junr	1480. Isaac Drake
1465. Wm.Rickey	1481. David Earhart
1466. Joseph Chumbly	1482. Elijah Earhart
1467. Benjamin Bashaw	1483. Isaac Birdwell
1468. Thomas Thomas	1484. Wm.Jackson
1469. Stephen White	1485. Daniel Young
1470.Alexander Ewing	1486. John L. Young
1471. James Ewing	1487. Wm.Short
1472. Barnabas Boils	1488. Wm.Perham (Parham ?)
1473. John Boils (?Bails)	1489. Christian Rasor
1474. Chraitopher Elmore	1490. John Cridcle
1475. John Duffell	1491. Matthew Patterson
1476. John Wilson	1492. John Patterson
1477. Buchanan Linear	1493. Stuart Fambrough.

1494. Thomas Parker	1509. Tilford Reading
1495. George Birdwell	1510. Joseph Hooper
1496. Britain Harper	1511. Rubin Bigs
1497. Robert Taylor	1512. John Clay
1498. Stephen Johnston	1513. Thomas Taylor, Senr
1499. Thomas Ozburn	1514. Thomas Taylor, Junr
1500. Absolom Page	1515. Isaac Beasley
1501. Vinson Page	1516. Peter Bashaw
1502. John Page	1517. James T.Beasley
1503. Wm.Wallace	1518. Samuel Love
1504.David Parker	1519. Joseph Love.
1505. Jesse Parker	
1506. Benjamin Branch	
1507. Robert Reading	
1508. Augustus Reading	

----------In   Captain Campbell's Militia Company.------

1520. Shedrack Bell	1547. Samuel Overton
1521. James Cooper	1548. Wm.Dickson
1521. Laban Barker	1549. John Coots
1522. David Beaty	1550. Morris Garrett
1523. Wm.Beaty	1551. John McEwen
1524. Josiah Phalps	1552. Nathaniel Brown
1525. Lewis Sturdivan	1553. Martin Adams
1526. Jesse Maxell (Maxwell)	1554. Nathaniel Tatum
1527. Allen Cotton	1555. Robert Adams
1528. Andrew Lucas	1556. Benjamin Lenear
1529. Thomas Malone	1557. Nathan Ewing
1530. Richard Matthews	1558. Joseph Seales (?Scales)
1531. John Murdock	1559. Turner Davis
1532. Andrew Cassellman	1560. William Nicholson
1533. Alexander Campbell	1561. Jesse Wharton
1534. Francis Campbell	1562. Thomas Smith
1535. Philip Campbell	1563. Roger B. Sappington
1536. Philip Pipkins	1564. Robert Johnston
1537. Thomas Cox.	1565. Armistead Johnston
1538. John Lucas	1566. Bennett Williams
1539. Sylvenus Cassellman	1567. Robert Cartwright
1540. Thomas Garrett	1568. Thomas Broadnax
1541. Henry Barnes	1569. George Bell
1542. John McCutchen	1570. David Taitt
1543. Joseph Coldwell	1571. Lemon Barker
1544. Hugh McCrory	1572. Wm.Thomas
1545. Peter Randolph	1573. Jarrott Nelson
1546. John Overton	1574. Wm. Bumpson (Bumpass ?)

1575. Wm.Howlett
1576. Sion Smith
1577. Henry Cobler (Cabler)
1578. Harris Cobler (Cabler)
1579. Christopher Cobler
1580. Joseph Austin
1581. John Alfred
1582. Nicholas Cobler
1583. Solomon Holder
1584. Thomas Brown
1585. Andrew Wilson
1586. John Bradford
1587. Joshua Curtis
1588. Wm.Harris
1589. Robert Hart
1590. John Wharton
1591. David Cartwright

1592.John Goodman
An additional list by Benijah
Gray issued.
1593. Ruben Cox.
1594. John Fly
1595. Wm. Drake
1596. Frederick Thompson
1597. Jacob Morton
1598. Charles Johnston
1599. James Blakely
1600. Enoch Ensley

--------------In Captain   McCormack's Militia Company ----

1601. John Carney
1602. Peter Douge
1603. Alexander Gower
1604. Wm.Willy
1605. Daniel Dunn
1606. Thomas Haile
1607. John Hupper (Hooper'
       or Hupper)
1608. Lewis H. Lee
1609. Elijah Spilman
1610. Nicholas Young
1611. Abraham Tippey
1612. Elisha Gower
1613. Benjamin Moss
1614. Robert Gower
1615. Russell Gower
1616. John Luthert ?
1617. John Lee, Senr.
1618. Braxton Lee
1619. Maxwell Hunter
1620. Henry Lee
1621. David S. Ethrige
1622. Charles Stuart
1623. John Cagle
1624. Nichol Dull
1625. Wm.Carney
1626. Wm.McCormack
1627 Felix Demumbrn
1628. George McCormack
1629. Joseph Derratt
1630. Rollen Felts
1631. Wm.Felts.

1631. Wm. Felts
1632. Wm. Bottee
1633. Thomas Maness (?)
1634. George Felts
1635. Lewis Mannss
1636. Thomas Felts
1637. Wm. Simmons
1638. John S.McCormack
1639. Wm.Haile
1640. John Duncan
1641. Adam Binkley
1642. Charles Cagle
1643. Bartlett Baw   ??
1644. Thomas Crain
1645. Jeremiah Daniel
1646. Dasdel Daniel
1647. Barton Daniel
1648. Augustus Reddin
1649. Elisha Piland.
1650. Thomas Lins ?
1651. John Hail
1652. Shedrack Miller
1653. Peter Binkley
1654. John Lee, Jr.
1655. Frederick Binkley
1656. Adam Binkley Junr
1657. Charles Green
1658. Matthias Parks
1659. Augustus Reddin Jr
1660. Thomas Boyt

--------- In Captain Belk's Militia Company ----------

1661. Cary Felts	1711. Hosea Boswell
1662. Robert Buchanan	1712. Miles Boswell
1663. Henry Bennett.	1713. Ed Collingsworth
1664. James Blair	1714 Joseph Wright
1665. Wm.Bibby	1715. Yancey B. Ham
1666. Wm.Matlock	1716. Charles Hayes
1667. Charles Cruchfield	1717 Samuel Ford
1668. Joseph Smith	1718. Linton Haile
1669. Dennis McLindon	1719. Thomas Joyce
1670. John Sluder	1720. Wm.Murphey
1671.Francis Sanders	1721. Daniel Valux
1672. James Howell	1722. James Campbell
1673. James Wright	1723. James Campbell.
1674. William Wright	1724 Green Seat
1675. George Wright	1725. Thomas Buchanan
1676. John Gower (Gowers ?)	1726. Jesse Fly
1677. Wm Shelby	1727. Robert Orr
1678.Peter Wright	1728. Washington Charlton
1679.Seth Webber	1729. John Moore
1680. Bird Evans	1730. Richard Moore
1681. Thomas Golden	1731. Wm·Wright
1682. Henry White Senr	1732. Joseph Seate
1683. Henry White Junr	1733. Truman Crenshaw
1684. Asa White	1734. Wm.H.McLaughlin
1685. George Hartman	1735. Samuel Bell.
1686. Wm.Gowans	1736. James Bell
1687. Wm.P. Seate	1737, John Bell
1688. George Hamilton	1738. John Herberson
1689. Joseph Bennett	1739. Levi Joiner
1690. Wm.Cropper	1740 Charlton Joiner
1691. Henry Seat	1741.Thomas White
1692. Little B. Williams	1742. Joseph Taylor
1693. Nathaniel Way	1743. John Harmon
1694. Wm.Hayes	1744. Caleb Zachary
1695. Jeremiah Ezzell	1745. Moses Jones
1697. Robert Bell	1746. Wm.Finney
1698. Thomas Bell.	1747. John Allen
1699. Wm.Bell	1748. Benjamin Allen
1700. Wadkins Brown	
1701. Thomas Neal	NOTE: 1796 Was missed in the
1702. Godfrey Shelton	numbering in the original.
1703. James Hamilton	There were two 1705. ERW
1704. Joseph Seat	
1705. George Hamilton	
1705. Robert Wayte	
1706. Alexander McCombs	
1707. James Finney	
1708. Andrew Finney	
1709. Henry Mise	
1810. James Glasgow,	

--------In Captain Roger's Old Militia Company -----

1749. Frederick Stump	1800. John Clevis
1750. John Stump	1801. Wm. W. Hudnell
1751. Lawrence McCormack	1802. Wm.Douglass
1752. Neal Watkins	1803. Wm. Caldwell
1753. Roger McDaniel	1804. Wm. Anderson
1754. Lewis Earthman	1805. John Counsellman (?Cassell-
1755. Peter Harrington	man)
1756. Wm.Turner	1806. George Cagle
1757. Henry Adcock	1807. Stephen Catender
1758. Meshack Haile	1808. Wm.Ritchey
1759. Isaac Earthman	1809. Henry Douglass
1760. Wm.Paradise	1810. Alexander Lester
1761. Mark Witaker (Whitaker)	1811. Wm. Wallace Jr.
1762. Wm.Merryman	1812. John Criddle
1763. Henry Raner	1813. Wm.Cleaves (?Gleaves)
1764. Jeffrey Johnston	1814. John Brown
1765' Thomas Douglass	1815. Zeris Tate
1766. Alexander Douglass	1816. Cornelius Manly
1767. Martin Garrett	1817. Wm.Evans
1768. Benjamin Drake	1818. Frederick Miller
1769. Isaac Drake	1819. Littleton Green
1770. John Drake	1820. Buchanan Lenear
1771.	1821. Edward Donnell
1772. Wm. Craddock	1822. Christopher Stump
1773. Robert Heaton	1823. Christopher Elmore
1774. Wm.Drake	1824. Wm.David (or Davis)
1775. Benjamin Drake Junr	1825. Daniel Young
1776. Jesse Drake	1826. John L. Young
1777. Levi Morgan	1827. John Mosier
1778. Jesse Smith	1828. Wm.Homes
1779. Benjamin Smith	1829. David Abernathy
1780. Jabez Catto	1830. Wm.Jones
1781. Asa Pace	1831. Henry Gingrick
1782. Henry Goldberry	1832. Alexander Ewing
1783. Abraham Nowlen	1833. Wm.Fugus
1784. Wm. Murrell	1834. James Glenn
1785. Laban Abernathy Junr	1835. David Wills (Wells)
1786. Laban Abernathy Senr	1836. John D. Johnston
1787. Nelson Lowrt	1837. Cuddy Harris
1788. Thomas Lovell	1838. Frederick Clayton
1789. Christopher Waggoner	1839. Wm.Ridge
1790. John Waggoner	1840. David Caldwell
1791. Jacob Waggoner	1841. Wm.Caldwell
1792. Cornelius Waggoner	1842. Thomas Lenns ?
1793. Jonis Fox	1843. John Linn
1794. Wm.Gilbert	1844. Christian Rasor
1795. Jones Read	184 . Frederick Fisher
1796. Joseph Yarbrough	1845. Elisha Carney
1797. Wm.Parram	1846. Vincent Carney
1798. Joseph Chumbly	1847. James Crosslen
1799. John G. Blithe	1848. Clayborn Gentry.

1849. John Gentry
1850. John Skinner
1851. Thomas Green
1852. August McRivers
1853. John B. Dillon
1854. James Shivers ?
1855. Westley Halson
1856. John Blair
1857. Mastin Cain
1858. Joseph Lark (Tark ?)
1859. Daniel Fowler.

1860. John Warden
1861. Alley Fergison
1862. Elijah Garrison
1863. Wm.Short
1864. Stephen White
1865. Joseph Gray
1866. Nicholas Tull
1867. John Shield
1868. David C. Faguin
1869. John Miller

NOTE: 1771 is out of the original. Numbered, skipped
1845 but listed a name. These irregularities concur with
the original record. ERW
----------IN CAPTAIN McADAMS MILITIA COMPANY _____

1870. Paul Dismukes
1871. John Dismukes
1872. John Boyd
1873. Greenwood Payne
1874. Squar Payne
1875. George Payne
1876. Joseph Payne
1877. Rauben Payne
1878. Andrew Davis
1879. Blackamore Davis
1880. Henry Booth Senr
1881. Henry Booth Junr
1882. Jacob Howson
1883. James Byrns, Senr
1884. Wm. Byrns
1885. James Byrns Junr
1886. George Perry
1887. Almore Walker
1888.
1889. Abraham Alules ?
1890. Mannassch Logue
      Wm.R. McAdams.
1891. Robert Davis
1892. Wm.Williams
1893. Wm.Baker
1894. Joseph Williams
1895. Wm.P.Bowers
1896. John Gilbreath
1897. Wiley Cooke
1898. Ephraim Manner
1899. James Guelliford
1900. John Conger
1901. David Louge
1902. Thomas Dorris
1903. Thomas Sparkman

1904. Alimelick Harrin (Herrin or
      Harris)
1905. Beverly Harrin (Herrin or
      Harris)
1906. Nicholas Crossway
1907. James Williamson
1908. George Campbell
1909. Greenberry Randal
1910. Frederick Lassitor
1911. Edwin S.Moore
1912. Zachariah Betts
1913. Robert Bates
1914. George Pirtle
1915. John Pirtle
1916. Hesse Glasgow
1917. John Underwood
1918. Ephraim Harris (?)
1919. Charles Cooper
1920. Andrew McCormick
1921. Thomas Ragan
1922. Benjamin Ragan
1923. Dempsey Powell
1924. Allen Matthis
1925. Wm.Dorris
1926. Laughlin McLand
1927. Wm.Campbell
1928. John Orr
1929. Wm.Hackney
1930. Lewis Carter
1931. Richard Harmon.
1932. Wm.Hughbanks
1933. Aquilla Randal
1934. Wm.Watts
1935. Joel Cook
1936. Wm.Watson.

1937. Peter Bezer	1952 Joshua Drake
1938. Jeptha Rice	1953. Joseph Perry
1939. Lemuel Bowers	1954. John Blake
1940. James Conger	1955. Shaven Dorris
1941. Thomas Rower	1956. Andrew Booth
1942. Ruben Cook	1957.Wm.Foster
1943. George McCormack	1958. Carlos Louge
1944. John McCormack	1959. Wm.Owen
1945. John Willard	1960.Isaac Davis
1946. Levi Dorris	1961.Samuel Tenning ?
1947. Thomas Cartwright	1962. Hugh Williams
1948.Jesse Hackney	1963. Wm.Donelson
1949. Charles Byrn	
1950.Isaac Reeder	
1951.Lewis Bracy	

-------In Captain Winfrey's Militia Company ------------

1964. Wm.Hudson	1998. Matthew Allen
1965. James H.Gamble	1999. Valentine Winfrey
1966. John Pride	2000. Jeremiah Hinton
1967. Francis McKay	2001. John Brackin
1968. Zach Stull	2002. Robert Weakley
1969. Wm.McSeay	2003. Moody Harris
1970. Samuel Weakley	2004. Thomas Patterson
1971.Paul Vaughn	2005. James Maury
1972. Wm.Philips	2006. Wm.Maury
1973. Carter Allen	2007. John Nichols
1974. David Vaughn	2008. Elisha Williams
1975. Samuel Edgar	2009. Joshua A. Parker
1976. Craven Weaver	2010. Washington Perkins
1977. Hugh Kerr	2011. Wm.Perkins.
1978. Amos Willis	2012. David Perkins
1979. Elisha Williams	2013. Abraham Perkins
1980. Josiah Williams	2014. John Philips
1981. William Williams	2015. Richard Harmand
1982. Daniel Dismukes	2016. Simon Everrett
1983. Wm.Ferguson	2017. Azariah Long
1984. Henry F. Yates	2018. George Birdwell
1985. Isaac Clemmons	2019. Hugh Birdwell
1986. Archibald H.Harris	2020. Isaac Birdwell
1987. Shedrack Cayce	2021. Wm.Willis
1988. John Dotson	2022. Samuel M.Cox
1989. Wm.Hugins	2023. Wm.Maxey
1990. Geo Blankenship	2024. John Maxey
1991. Henry S. Allen	2025. Bennett Maxey
1992. James P. McReard ?	2026. James Maxey
1993. Edward Hudgins	2027. Wm.Scott
1994. Alexander Fergison	2028. Thomas Miles
1995. Abraham Starking ?	2029. John Moore
1996. James Hudgins	2030. Wm.Jackson
1997. Wm. Nash	2031. Alexander McDowel

2032. Oliver Johnston	2043. James Lemmons
2033. Joseph Rurff	2044. James B.Moore
2034. John Chapman	2045. Wm.W. Ray Senr
2035. Benjamin Pattison	2046. George Smith
2036. Edmond Gamble	2047. John C. Parker
2037. Wm.Ballew	2048. David Parker
2038. Wm.Hobson	2049. Jesse Parker
2039. John Hobson	2050. Wm.Parker.
2040 Isaac Hudson	
2041. John Robertson	
2042. David Pulley	

------In Captain Bening's Militia Company ------------

2051. Thomas Thornburgh	2089. John Allen
2052. George M.Martin	2090. Thomas Hill
2053. Peter Bass	2091. Charles Cassady
2054. Henry Dauty	2092. Lanier Cooper
2055. John Waggoner	2093. George Poyzer
2056. Robert Dodd	2094. James Bening
2057. Wm.L. Yarbrough	2095. Alexander Porter
2058. Richard B. Owen	2096. Thomas Claiborne
2059, Lewis Harrison	2097. Patrick Bigley
2060. George Martin	2098. James Young
2061. James Davis	2099. Hensen Hardy
2062. Josephus Taylor	2100. Charles Bowers
2063. Lawson Berry	2101. John Woodcock
2064. John Berry	2102. Joseph Bair ?
2065. Wm. Willis	2103. Allen Richardson
2066. James Taylor	2104. Clayton Talbott
2067. Burwell Sneed	2105. Wm.Garret
2068. Richard Pryor	2106. Caleb Maning
2069. John Rogers	2107. Wm.Mannly
2070. Thomas Connelly	2108. Archibald Dewel
2071. Lewis Speice ?	2109. Richard Garrett
2072. David Kaswtz	2110. Archibald Gray
2073. Wm.T.Halley	2111. John Newam (Newman ?)
2074. Thomas Hardy	2112. Charles Hartley.
2075. Wm.Kent	2113. Bauldy Vaughn
2076. Edward Cahall	2114. John M. Caffey
2077. Hardress Cane	2115. Daniel McBean
2078. Alexander Laird	2116. Boyd McNairy
2079. Wm.L.Boyd	2117. Wm.Taitt
2080 Samuel Goode	2118. Robert Stothart
2081. George Pence	2119. James Roan
2082. Bignal Crook	2120. Felix Grundy
2083. Peter Johnston	2121. Nathaniel McNairy
2084. Wm.Connelly Senr	2122. Oliver B. Hayes
2085. Wm.Connelly Junr.	2123. Samuel Haney
2086. Matthew Brooke	2124. Jesse Sutton
2087. James Page	2125. Henry Questenberry
2088. Bernard Hagans	2125. Joseph Coleman

2126. **Hugh Haddon**
2127
2128. **Richard Outlaw**
2129. James Priestly
2130. Wm.Hume
2131. John Caulfield
2132. Wm.Westley
2133. James Davis
2134. Edmond Harrison
2135. Levi Claybrooks
2136. John Kent
2137. Phillip Thomas
2138. Henry C.Ewing
2139. Andrew Ewing.

2140. **Wm. Lytle**
2141. **Wm.B.Lewis**
2142. John Strother.

NOTE: The numbers do not run accurate in the original, so are given here as in the original. ERW

-------- **In Captain Trigg and Moses Militia Company** -----

2143. Wm.R. Evans
2144. Huston Cooper
2145. Henry Cooper
2146. Micajah Busby
2147. Robert Busby
2148. Ezekiel Douglass
2149. Daniel Martin
2150. John Anderson
2151. Robert Anderson
2152. Thomas Sadler
2153. Abraham Smith
2154. Eli Smith
2155. Jesse Shelton
2156. Wm.Harwood
2157. John Harwood
2158. Wm.Reaves
2159. James Reaves
2160. Philip Cloyd
2161. Allen Thompson
2162. Thomas Beamer
2163. Daniel Joslin Senr
2164. Samuel Joslin
2165. James Joslin
2166. Wm.Scott
2167. Wm.Thompson
2168. Thomas Scott
2169. John E.Clark
2170. James Mathis
2171. John Cooper
2172. Wm.G.Wilkerson
2173. Daniel Sullivan
2174. Neal Thompson
2175. Francis Mothershed
2176. Wm.Nelson
2177. Henry McElwand

2178 John Cooke
2179. Booker Richardson
2180. Maliohy Lile
2181. George Lile
2182. Daniel McDaniel
2183. Jacob Suggs
2184. George Wair
2185. George Locke
2186. Wm.Fowler
2187. Samuel Nicholass
2188. Jesse Cox
2189. Wm.B.McDaniel
2190. Benjamin Woodard
2191. Wm.Newland
2192. Wm.Aaron
2193. Thomas Shuder
2194. Aaron Baldwin
2195. Pleasant Tally
2196. Wm.Francis
2197. John Stonett
2198. Leonard F.Piles
2199. John Simmons
2200. Moses Baldwin
2201. George Thunderbark
2202. Jonathan Johnston
2203. Robert Swingfellow
2204. Williamson Harper
2205. Jeremiah Baxter
2206. Josiah Landrum
2207. Edward Mobley
2208. Butler Noles
2209. Corbin Noles
2210. Thomas Allen
2211. Gustavus Rape
2212. Henry Rape

2213. Henry Thunderback
2214. Wm.B.Evans
2215. Wm.H. Stennitt
2216. Wm.Herrin
2217. Leonard Burnett
2218. James D.Sharp
2219. Joseph Neely.
2220. Sheppard Landrum
2221. Theodore Hunt
2222. John Ivey
2223. Frances Tatom
2224. Wm.Tatham (Latom ?)

2225. Daniel Joslin Jur
2226. Bird Joslin
2227. James McEwing
2228. M.C. Dunn
2229. George Johnston
2230. Nathaniel Curtis
2231. Wm.Wallace Senr
2232. Green Payne.

N.B. It is to be noticed that several of the Entrys Possess the same number and that the correct numbers is 2235 as appears on Comparing the Originals & C.

The book record from which this list has been taken carried the above N.B. at the end. The original rolls are not available, but fortunately the lists were copied in the record book. The record book was of very very thin paper and is fast crumbling.

* * * * * * * * * * * *

RECORD OF COMMISSIONS OF OFFICERS IN THE

TENNESSEE MILITIA 1811.

DAVIDSON COUNTY REGIMENTS ONLY

John Allen, Ensign 19th Regiment, Commissioned
July 17, 1811

Latten F. Allen, Captain. 19th Regiment. Commissioned
May 25, 1811.

William Allen, Lieutenant 19th Regiment. Commissioned
July 17, 1811

William S. Allen, Captain 19th Regiment. Commissioned
July 17, 1811.

John Barnhart, Captain 19th Regiment, Commissioned
May 25, 1811.

Edward Bondurant, Captain in Volunteer Rifle Company
19th Regiment, Commissioned Sept. 17, 1811

James Booth, Captain 20th Regiment, Commissioned
Feby 5, 1811.

James R.Bosley, Lieutenant in Volunteer Rifle
Company 19th Regiment. Commissioned Sept. 17, 1811.

Thomas G. Bradley, First Major 19th Regiment,
commissioned Jany 17, 1811

Isaac Butler, Captain 20th Regiment, Commissioned
June 22, 1811.

William Carrell. Captain in the Independent
Company (Blues) 19th Regiment. Commissioned May 25, 1811.

William J.Davis, Ensign 20th Regiment. Commissioned
Nov. 9, 1811.

Samuel Dennis, Ensign 19th Regiment,Commissioned July
17, 1811.

Archibald Deval, Ensign, 19th Regiment. Commissioned
July 17, 1811.

Jack Dickinson, Leiuetnant, 20th Regiment, Commissioned, Nov. 9, 1811.

Lewis Dillahunt (Dullahunty) Ensign 19th Regiment,
commissioned, April 19, 1811.

William Drake, Captain 20th Regiment. Commissioned Nov. 9, 1811

Rodney Earheart, Lieutetant 20th Regiment. Commissioned Nov.9, 1811

Anthony C.Foster, Leiutenant, 19th Regiment. Commissioned May 25, 1811

Moses Fowler, Ensign 20th Regiment, Commissioned Nov. 9, 1811.

John Frazier, Lieutenant 20th Regiment, Commissioned June 22, 1811.

James Freeland, Lieutehant, 19th Regiment , commissioned July 17, 1811.

Archibald H.Harris, Lieutenant, 20th Regiment, commissioned Nov. 9, 1811.

Edward D. Hobbs, Captain 19th Regiment. Commissioned, July 17, 1811.

Etheldred Horne, Captain 20th Regiment, Commissioned Nov. 9, 1811.

Robert Johnson, Second Major 19th Regiment, was commissioned Jany 17, 1811.

Littleberry Lassesure, Lieutenant 19th Regiment. Commissioned July 17, 1811.

William R. McAdams, Captain 20th Regiment.Commissioned Nov. 9, 1811

John McCormack, Captain 20th Regiment, Commissioned Nov. 9, 1811.

John McElwain, Lieutenant 19th Regiment. Commissioned Aug.22, 1811.

James Mitchell, Ensign, 20th Regiment. Commissioned June ,22, 1811.

James Murry, Ensign 20th Regiment, Commissioned Nov. 9, 1811.

John Napier, Ensign 19th Regiment, Commissioned July 17, 1811.

William Nelms, Ensign, 20th Regiment.Commissioned Nov. 9, 1811.

Robert Newton, Ensign 19th Regiment, Commissioned April 19, 1811.

John Oar (Orr), Lieutenant 20th Regiment, Commissioned Feby 5, 1811.

John C. Parker, Second Major 20th Regiment. Commissioned July 27, 1811.

Joshua Paxton, Lieutenant in the Independent Company (Blues) 19th Regiment. Commissioned May 25, 1811

Philip Pepkin, Lieutenant Col. Commandant, 19th Regiment, Commissioned Jany 17, 1811.

John Rogers, Ensign 19th Regiment, May 25, 1811. date of Commission.

Thomas Shepherd, Ensign in Volunteer Rifle Company 19th Regiment, Commissioned Sept. 17, 1811.

Peton (Peyton) Smith, Lieutenant 19th Regiment, Commissioned April 19, 1811.

John Stump, Lieutenant Colonel Commandant 20th Regiment, Commissioned July 27, 1811.

Robert Stringfellow, Captain 19th Regiment, commissioned Aug. 22, 1811.

Wilkins Tannehill, Ensign in the Independent Company (Blues) 19th Regiment. Commissioned May 25, 1811.

Samuel Taylor, First Major 20th Regiment, Commissioned July 27, 1811.

Austin M.Wade, Lieutenant 19th Regiment, Commissioned May 25, 1811.

George Waggoner, Lieutetant 20th Regiment. Commissioned Nov. 9, 1811.

Thomas B.White, Ensign, 19th Regiment. Commissioned Aug. 25, 1811.

Valentine Winfree, Captain 20th Regiment. Nov. 9, 1811 date of commission.

Nicholas Young, Lieutenant, 20th Regiment. Commissioned Nov. 9, 1811.

William Baker, Lieutenant of Cavalry 9th Brig.Commissioned March 14, 1812.

James Benning, Captain 19th Regiment. Commissioned
Feb.11, 1812

Hugh Birdwell, Captain 20th Regiment,Commissioned,
April 29, 1812

Richard Boyd,   Captain 20th Regiment,Commissioned
March 24, 1812

David S. Deadrick, Lieutenant in Company of
Republican Blues attached to 19th Regiment, Commissioned
Dec. 3, 1812.

Allen Dotson, Lieutenant 19th Regiment. Commissioned
April 16, 1812

John Drury, Lieutenant 19th Regiment, Commissioned
March 24, 1812

Thomas Edmiston, Leiuetant of Cavalry 9th Bridage,
commissioned Dec. 18, 1812.

Andrew J. Edmuston, Cornet of oavalry,9th Regiment,
commissioned July 12, 1812.

John Gwin, Lieutenant 19th Regiment, Commdssioned
Sept. 12, 1812

Collin S.Hobbs, Ensign 19th Regiment, Commissioned
Sept. 12, 1812.

Absalom Hooper, Lieutenant in Capt. Stump's Volunteer troops of Cavalry, 9th Brigade. Commissioned Aug.1,1812.

Charles Johnston, Ensign 19th Regiment, July 1, 1812
date of Commission.

William Kent, Lieutenant 19th Regiment, Commissioned
Feby 11, 1812

Buchannon Lanier, Ensign in Capt. Stump's Company
of Mounted Infantry attached to 20th Regiment, Commissioned
Sept. 15, 1812.

John B.Long, Major of 7th Brig, Commissioned Sept.18,
1812.

William McAdams, Lieutenant 20th Regiment, Commissioned
April 29, 1812.

James McCutcheon, Captain,Regiment of Cavalry 9th
Brigade. Commissioned July 1, 1812.

William McMurry, Ensign 19th Regiment, Commissioned
March 24, 1812.

George J.Martin, Ensign 19th Regiment, commissioned
July 1, 1812

John Moore, Ensign, 19th Regiment, Commissioned
July 13, 1812

Thomas B. Pipkin, Ensign 19th Regiment,Commissioned
Dec. 3, 1812.

Benjamin Rogan, Ensign 20th Regiment, Commissioned
May 26, 1812.

David Richardson, Captain 19th Regiment, Commissioned
April 16, 1812.

John Rogers, Lieutenant 19th Regiment, Commissioned
July 13, 1812

Thomas Rutherford, First Major of Cavalry, 9th
Brigade, Commissioned April 3, 1812

James Sitler, Ensign in Company of Republican Blues
attached to 19th Regiment. Commissioned Dec. 12, 1812.

Richard Stringfellow, Ensign 19th Regiment, Commissioned April 16, 1812.

Jesse W.Thomas, Captain 19th Regiment, Commissioned
Feby 11, 1812.

William Valux, Ensign 19th Regiment. Commissioned
July 13, 1812.

George Whitson, Lieutenant 19th Regiment, Commissioned
March 24, 1812.

George W.Wolf, Lieutenant 10th Regiment. Commissioned
July 1, 1812.

Peter Wright, Captain, 19th Regiment. Commissioned
March 24, 1812.

* * * * * * * * * *

<u>MISC. Data regarding some commissioned officers.</u>

Captain James Kincade (KinKade) was commissioned a
Captain 19th Regiment, July 23,1810.

Captain Isaac Butler was commissioned a Captain   of
the 20th Regiment, June 22, 1811.

Captain Richard Boyd, was commissioned March 24, 1812
as Captain of 19th Regiment.

Captain _____Williamson. There was in Davidson
County, John Williamson who was commissioned Captain May 10,
1797. Also Thomas Williamson who was commissioned Lieutenant
First Regiment, Davidson County, Jany 9, 1800, and to Captain
First Regiment, Sept. 29, 1800. John S.Williamson was commissioned Lieutenant 19th Regiment, July 24, 1807 Davidson
County.   John Williamson received a commission as Captain of
the Independent Company 19th Regiment, April 25, 1809, Davidson County. Joseph N.Williamson was commissinned Lieutenant
19th Regiment, April 18, 1809. Joseph N.Williamson was commissioned Captain 19th Regiment July 23, 1810.

George Hail was commissioned Captain 19th Regiment
July 8, 1808. Davidson County.

Captain William Mullens received his commission as
Captain, Davidson County. 29th Regiment. Aug. 29, 1810.

David Cloyd was commissioned a Captain 20th Regiment,
August 15, 1809, Davidson County.

William Henny (Henry), received a commission as
Captain 19th Regiment. Jany 10, 1810.

Henry Liles was commissioned a Captain 19th Regiment
Davidson County,July 21, 1809.

Dempsey Morris, was commissioned Ensign 20th Regiment,
March 5, 1808 Davidson County. He was commissioned Captain
20th Regiment, July 21, 1809 and also Aug. 15,1809 is a
record of his commission as Captain. Daddon.

William Creels was commissinned a Captain 19th
Regiment, Davidson County,July 21, 1809.

Hugh Birdwell was commissioned Lieutenant
20th Regiment, Feby 11,1809 Davidson County, and was commissione
Captain 20th Regiment April 29, 1812.

There was a David Campbell who received a Commission
as Ensign, First Regiment , in Davidson County, Aug.16, 1798
Philip Campbell was commissioned Lieutenant of 19th Regiment

Nov. 7 ,1807 Davidson County. Then Philip Campbell was
commissioned Captain 19th Regiment, Feby 20, 1810 Davidson Co.

John Rogers, in Davidson County, was commissioned a
Lieutenant 20th Regiment, April 12, 1810; Also Commissioned
Lieutenant 19th Regiment July 23, 1810; The there was a William
Rogers commissioned Lieutenant 20th Tegiment, Feby 20,1810;
William W. Rogers was commissioned Captain 20th Regiment, April
12, 1810 , and John Rogers, received a commission as Ensign
19th Regiment, May 25, 1811.

Valentine Winfree was commissioned Captain 20th
Regiment, Davidson County, May 21, 1808. A man of the same
name (maybe same man) was Commissioned Captain 20th Regiment
Nov. 9,1811 Davidson County.

PENSION AGENTS IN TENNESSEE 1834.

Senate Document June 5, 1834, shows the following as
Pension agents in Tennessee.

Charles T.Porter;   Tennessee.
Stephen Cantrill,   Nashville, Tennessee.
Thomas Crutcher.   Nashville, Tennessee
Luke Lea, Knoxville, Tennessee.
Robert King,. Knoxville, Tennessee.
Wm.K.Blair. Jonesboro, Tennessee.

POST OFFICES IN DAVIDSON COUNTY, 1857
Chestnut Grove........ James H. Fulghum postmaster.
Elm Hill, James H.Charlton, postmaster
Franklin College, Tolbert Fanning, Postmaster
Goodlettsville, John H. Galbreath, Postmaster
Hamilton's Creek, Elmore C.Rowe, Postmaster.
Marrowbone, Jackson Crockett, Postmaster
Nashville, Samuel R. Anderson. Postmaster
Ridge Post, Wilkins T.Garrett, Postmaster
South Harpeth, Thomas I.Allison. Postmaster
Stewart's Ferry, Benjamin Hurt, Postmaster
Sycamore Mills, Randolph Simmons, Postmaster
Tank, Joseph H.Dillahunty, Postmaster
White Bend, P.M.Wade, Postmaster.

AMERICAN STATE PAPERS---MILITARY AFFAIRS, VOLUME 7

WEST POINT MILITARY ACADEMY FROM TENNESSEE, 1835

This list covers the period from 1814 to 1835, and is most interesting.

William B. McClellan, admitted 1815 from Tennessee, withdraw in 1819.

E.G.W. Butler, admitted 1816, from Tennessee, graduated in 1820.

Alexander Barron, admitted 1816, withdrew, 1818. frpm Tennessee.

John J.Abercrombie, admitted 1817, from Tennessee, Graduated in 1822.

Richard Cross, admitted 1817, withdraw 1819, from Tennessee.

A.J.Donelson, admitted 1817. from Tenn. Graduated 1820.

Samuel Kennedy, admitted 1817, from Tenn. withdrew 1819.

Marcus Anderson admitted 1818 from Tenn. withdrew 1819.

N.W. Easterland admitted 1818 from Tenn. Withdrew, 1820.

Albert S.Miller, admitted 1818, from Tenn. Graduated 1823.

D.M. Porter, admitted 1818 from Tenn. Graduated 1821.

D.S. Donelson, admitted 1821, from Tenn. Graduated 1825.

J.Meredith, admitted 1821 from Tenn. withdrew -----

James Allison, admitted 1822, from Tenn. dismissed in 1825.

James G.Allen, admitted 1822, from Tenn. graduated 1825.

P.B.Anderson, admitted from Tenn. 1823, withdrew 1825

Samuel J.Hayes, admitted from Tenn. 1823. withdrew 1826.

R.M. Saunders, admitted from Tenn 1823,withdrew 1823.

C.H.Watkins, admitted from Tenn. 1823.Dismissed 1824.

J.L. Dasheil, admitted from Tenn. 1824. Dismissed from the Academy in 1825.

J.G.M. Floyd, admitted from Tennessee, 1824,Dismissed from the Academy in 1825.

William Gellespie, admitted from Tenn. 1824, Dismissed 1825.

Joel Lewis, admitted from Tennessee, 1824,Mismissed from the Academy in 1825.

James Thompson, admitted from Tennessee 1824, Graduated in 1828.

Robert Serrin, admitted from Tennessee, 1824, Graduated in 1828.

W.D.Chappell, admitted 1825 from Tenn, withdrew in the same year.

J.G.M. Floyd, was admitted again in 1825 from Tenn, but in 1827 withdrew.

John Roberts, admitted from Tenn, 1825, withdrew in 1826.

J.T. Collinsworth, admitted in 1826, graduated 1830.

William Moore. admitted from Tenn. 1826. Dismissed from the Academy in 1828.

George W. Lawson was admitted from Tenn, in 1826, and graduated in 1830.

J.G. Overton was admitted from Tennessee in 1826. He died at the Academy in 1828.

C. Schoolfield,was admitted from Tenn, in 1826. Dismissed from the Academy in 1827.

J.L. Williams was admitted from Tenn in 1826 and withdrew the next year, 1827.

A.M.Lea was admitted from Tenn, in 1827 and graduated in 1831.

C.W. Nelson was admitted from Tenn. 1827, withdrew the same year.

R.G.Fain was admitted 1828 and graduated 1832.

John W. McCrabb admitted 1828, graduated 1833.

Josh D.McCann admitted 1828 from Tenn, and was Dismissed from the Academy in 1829.

Asbury Ury was admitted from Tennessee in 1828, and graduated in 1832

H.K. Yoakum was admitted from Tenn. 1828 and graduated in 1832.

DOTS AND DASHES OF INFORMATION.

The following bits of information from old Legislative petitions in the Tennessee State Archives. Pertain to Davidson County.

1798. John Gordon, Justice of the Peace.
1798. Election returns. Jas. Robertson, Elected as State Senator. Davidson County.

In 1799 the Tennessee Legislature, voted confirmation of marriages of 1785-1786 authority, State of Franklin, inhabitants of Washington County. This covered certain persons in Davidson County.

L801 Legislative papers, Tennessee, Nashville inhabitants, for bounty for cotton manufacture.

1801 Petition to the Legislature, Nashville inhabitants for forming infantry company.

In 1815 there was a change in the county line of Davidson County. This was the line between Davidson and Williamson Counties.

These old Legislative Petitions are extremely interesting for they usually have signed to them many names of persons residing within that county. Here is also a place that original signatures of those individuals may be found.

PENSION LIST FOR WEST TENNESSEE 1818

This list is not broken down to counties, the entire list is given, because so many of them at one time lived in Davidson County, and moved westward.

NAME	RANK	LINE SERVED IN
Francis Arnold	Private	Virginia
John Austin	Private	Virginia
David Adams	Private	North Carolina
Andrew Bay	Sergt.Major	North Carolina
Jesse Bryant	Private	Virginia
William Bryant	Private	Virginia
Philip Brittain	Private	North Carolina
David Benton	Private	North Carolina
John Brent	Private	Virginia
Squire Baker	Private	Mass.
Lance James Barnett	Private	South Carolina
Thomas Brannan	Private	North Carolina
David E. Brown	Private	North Carolina
John Baker	Private	Georgia
William Bratcher	Private	South Carolina
James Bagget	Private	South Carolina
Jeremiah Bently	Private	Virginia
Joshua Curtis	Lieut.	North Carolina
John Coalden	Private	Virginia
John Christian	Fife Major	North Carolina
James Curtis	Private	Virginia
John Carney	Private	North Carolina
Daniel Clower	Private	North Carolina
Jacob Caulk	Private	Delaware.
William Cain	Private	Virginia
William Douglass	Private	N.C. (Suspended)
Farroll, O'Neal Daily	Private	Virginia
James Davis	Private	Virginia
William Deakins	Private	Pennsylvania
Jesse Dodd	Private	North Carolina
David Dodd	Private	North Carolina
Samuel Davis	Private	North Carolina
Richard Dean	Private	North Carolina
Richard Eppes	Sergt	Virginia
Timothy Ezell	Private	North Carolina
Perry Floyd	Private	Virginia
Jonathan Faire	Private	Virginia
David Greats	Private	Virginia
Joel Gunter	Private	North Carolina
John Gibson	Private	Maryland
Thomas Gamble	Private	Virginia
William Gibson	Private	North Carolina
William Gillehan	Private	South Carolina
Clement Hall	Captain	North Carolina

Samuel Hogg	Lieut	Virginia
James Hungerfoot	Private-	Virginia
Stephen Handlin	Private	Pennsylvania
Robert Hays	Lieutenant	North Carolina
John Huggins	Private	South Carolina
Robert Hill	Private	Virginia
John Hall	Private	North Carolina
David Harris	Private	Virginia
Elisha E.Johnson	Private	South Carolina
Henry Jordan	Private	Virginia
Job Jenkins	Private	Virginia
Benjamin Johnson	Private	North Carolina
John Jackson	Private	South Carolina.
John Kennedy	Private	Virginia
James Kennedy	Sergeant	Maryland
John Lasley	Private	North Carolina
John Martin	Private	Wirginia
Thomas McLain	Private	Pennsylvania
Mark Mitchell	Private	Virginia
Luke Metheany	Private	Virginia
Lester Morris	Private	Virginia
Edmund May	Private	Virginia
Andrew M'Mahan	Private	Virginia
Jesse Meredith	Private	Virginia
Jarrott Nelson	Private	Virginia
James Norsworthy	Sergeant	North Carolina
George Oakley	Private	Stricken from roll Oct. 12,1819.not Continental
Molliston Perrigen	Private	Virginia
Thomas Poore	Private	North Carolina
Thomas Parker	Private	Virginia
Reuben Roberts	Private	North Carolina
Jesse Robertson	Private	North Carolina.
Thomas Rutherford	Private	North Carolina
Samuel Reeves	Private	
Philip Shackler	Private	
Jacob Slaughter	Private	
Caleb Smith	Private	
Robert Singleton	Private	
William Scally	Private	Virginia
Robert Stewart	Private	Maryland
John Sutherland	Private	North Carolina
Samuel Smith	Private	North Carolina
Micajah Sims	Private	Virginia
Moses Spencer	Private	Virginia
Samuel Sarrett	Private	North Carolina
Josiah Stafford	Private	North Carolina
Elijah Smith	Private	Virginia
John Sage	Private	Virginia
Joshua Smith	Private	Virginia
James Tatum	Lieutetant	North Carolina
Henry Thomas	Private	Virginia

SOME PENSIONERS ON THE 1832 LIST, DAVIDSON CO.

NOTE: I have not duplicated names that appear on
the 1818, 1840 list. ERW

Jesse Adams, drew pension in the Nashville Agency.

John Alford, age 74, served in Virginia line, drew
pension 1832.

John Anderson, age 76 when he applied for pension
and placed on the 1832 list. He served in the Virginia
line.

James Barnes, who served in the Virginia line, was
on the pension list 1832 age 74 years.

Lieutenant Adam Binkley, who rendered service in
North Carolina, and was listed on the pension list in 1832
giving his age as 94 years.

Henry Bonar, on the list of 1832 age 79, as having
served in Pennsylvania.

James Brown, age 75 shown on the list of 1832. He
served in Virginia.

Lieutenant Morgan Brown, rendered service in South
Carolina. His age in 1832 given as 77 years.

Moses Brown, age 82 in 1832 who saw service in South
Carolina.

Charles Dibrell, served in the Virginia line. His
name appears on the 1832 list age 77 years.

Isaac Barthman, age 84 years in 1832, served in
North Carolina.

Elisha Garland , whose age in 1832 was given as
72 years, served in North Carolina.

Claiborne Gentry, served in the State of North Carolina. In 1832 his age appears as 73 years.

Joseph Gilmore, was a soldier in the War of 1812.
His name appears on the 1828 list of pensioners. He was
transferred from South Carolina. He died Feb.23, 1825.

John Goodrich, Senior, age 77 in 1832, served in
Virginia.

Zerobabel Gray, age 75 years in 1832. Service in

North Carolina.

William Haygood,who had served in the State of North
Carolina, was aged 79 in 1832 when his name appears on the
pension list.

James Hooker, whose age was given as 70 years in 1832;
served in Virginia.

Jesse Hooper, was a Georgia soldier, On the list of 1832
his age was given as 76 years.

Jacob House, a soldier in the War of 1812, appears on
the Pension list of 1828.

William Hudgens, another War of 1812 soldier. Who
served in the Tennessee Volunteers. Pleased on pension and
listed on the list of 1828.

Edmund Jennings. In 1832 his age was given as 81 years
and his place of service "Virginia"

William Jewell, was in the North Carolina service.
In 1832 his age was given as 77 years.

Peter Lesley, age 73 years, on the list of 1832;
service in North Carolina.

Richard Martin, served in the Tennessee Volunteers
in the War of 1812. His name appears on the 1828 pension list.

Gideon Mills, Was a soldier in the War of 1812. His
name shows on the pension list of 1828.

Frederick Owen, was age 82 years and his name appears
on the 1832 list. He rendered service in the State of Virginia.

Thomas Patterson, who had served in Virginia, was
age 74 years in 1832.

Charles T. Reese, was a soldier of the War of 1812.
His name appears on the pension list of 1828.

Charles Rogers, A soldier of the War of 1812, was
placed on pension and his name is given in the 1828 list.

William Shaw, served in Virginia. In 1832 his age
was given as 73 years.

Robert Thomas, served in North Carolina. In 1832 his
age was given as 75 years.

Thomas Thompson, served in North Carolina. In 1832
his age given as 75 years.

David Wills, was a soldier in the war of 1812. His
name appears on the pension list of 1812.

* *

DAVIDSON COUNTY, TENNESSEE, PENSION LIST 1840

Norvell Lipscomb age 84 years, residing with James
Walker.

Perkinson Jackman, age 77 years, was living in his
own home it seems.

James Haley, age 84 years. He was living with James H.
Haley, therefore, it must have been his own home.

Peter Leslie, shown on earlier pension list as Peter
Lesley, was age 80 years.

Gideon Johnson, age 86 years, was residing with
George Chadwell. Relationship not shown.

James Barnes, age 79 years.

Nicholas Hale, age 78 years. He had come from East
Tennessee.

Frederick Cabler (sometimes found spelled Cobler)
whose age was 82 years was living with John Corbitt in the
9th Civil District of Davidson County.

Joseph Vick, age 78 years, was living in the Ninth
Civil District. (He was buried at Mill Creek Cemetery,
grave marked or restored by DAR.---ERW)

John Williamson, age 79, lived in the Tenth Civil
District of Davidson County, and drew pension.

John McCutchin (also found spelled McCutcheon)
age 87 resided in the Eleventh Civil District of the county.

William Watkins, age 85 years, residing with William
E. Watkins, in the Twelfth Civil District of the county.

Caleb Mason, was 87 years of age and was living with
John Davis in the Twelfeth Civil District of the county.

John Casey, age 78, lived with Charles S. Casey, in the
Eighteenth Civil District of Davidson County.

Isaiah Alley age 91 years, was living with Thomas Alley
in the Eighteenth Civil District of the county.

Peter Bashaw, age 78 years, lived in the Nineteenth Civil District of Davidson County.

Benjamin Morgan, age 78 years, was living in the 19th Civil District.

William Coats (sometimes spelled Cootes or Coots) was age 80 years. He was living with Beverly E.Coats in the 20th Civil District of the County.

John McCaslin, age 90 years, was living in the home of Joshua Drake in the Twenty-second Civil District of the County.

Thomas Hickman, age 78 years lived in the Twenty-Third Civil District of the county in 1840 and drew pension.

Thomas Douglass, age 84 years was a resident of the Twenty-fourth Civil District in 1840.

George Smith, age 80 years, also lived in the 24th Civil District of the county, in 1840.

DO YOU KNOW THESE ARE FACTS ABOUT DAVIDSON CO.

In 1857, the population of Nashville and adjoining suburbs, was more than 45,000 population. Nashville proper was said to have been 25,000. This did not include Edgefield. In 1853 South Nashville, which had not been a part of Nashville proper had a population of 3000. Edgefield was not included as a part of Nashville in the earlier days. In 1860 the population of Nashville is given as 37,000 including suburbs.

Ex- Governor AAron V. Brown, Secretary of the U.S. Navy, maintained his residence 3 miles on the Franklin Pike. This in 1857.

Fort Negley, before the Civil War, was known as St.Cloud's Hill, a beautiful wooded hill. The Fort was built in the fall of 1862 under the direction of Major-General James S. Negley of Pennsylvania. It is said that after the war, it was the headquarters of a band or robbers. Here they stored ammunition, and from a cellar in the Fort it is said, they dug a tunnel to the McNairy vault in the Old City Cemetery on Fourth Avenue South.

Fort Cosino (now the City Resevoir) was erected about the same time as Fort Negley. Fort Morton was on a hill Northwest of Fprt Casino;named in honor of James St.Clair Morton, Chief Engineer to Major General Negley. Fort Houston was on 16th Ave., near Broad.

PENSION LIST AS AUTHORIZED PUBLISHED FOR 1883.

Note: The United States Reports--- 47th Congress,
Second Series, Executive Document No.84. Published 1883.
part 5. No. 2078-2079-2080-2081 and 2082. This report
is given by States and under each State the counties are
separated,------ the number of pension, the post office
of each pensioner, Cause of pension, monthly rate (omitted
in this report in) and the date pension was allowed. The
application files in the National Archives in many instances
contain much genealogical information. Often pages from
Old Family Bibles are found included. They are not all for
the War of 1812, but cover other pensioners for other wars
also. A goodly number, in fact, the larger percent of them
are for 1812 soldiers and heir dependants, however, there
are exceptions. ------ERW

Thomas Powell, No.73110. Post Office Address,
Antioch. He received a fracture of the leg. Went on pension
October 1866.

Elizabeth Reding, No. 26732, Post Office Baker,
Widow of a soldier of the War of 1812. She was allowed pension
September 1879.

Elizabeth M. Jones, No. 21305. Postoffice also Baker,
She was a widow of a soldier of the War of 1812. She was
allowed a pension March 1879.

Angeline Binkley, No.166029. Postoffice was Belleview. She was a widow and was granted pension September 1874.

Courtney Sawyer, No.20324, whose postoffice was
Belleview. He served in the War of 1812. Pension allowed
1879.

Chloe B. Stockett, No. 28175. Post Office Belleview. Widow of soldier of War of 1812. Pension allowed
December 1879.

Polly Thornton, No.18621. Postoffice Belleview,
a widow of a soldier of the War of 1812. Pension allowed
February 1879.

David L. Qnaw, No. ___?___ , Postoffice Donelson.
Had idsease of the lungs, He was allowed pension but
the date is not shown in this list. Neither is his Pension
Number.

Sarah E. Standley, No.12296. Postoffice being
Edgefield. Widow of War 1812 soldier. She was allowed
pension November 1878.

Sophia E. Arendell, No.7426. Postoffice was Edgefield. She was a widow with two children. The date she was approved for pension not given.

Valerius Draine, No. 57148. Post office Edgefield Junction. He lost his arm above the elbow in servide. Granted Pension February 1866.

Malinda R. Bayles, No.23919. Postoffice Edgefield Junction. She was widow of a soldier of the War of 1812. Her pension was allowed May 1079!

Eliza Calthrop (Calthrap), No.12362, Postoffice Goodlettsville. Widow of War of 1812, was allowed a pension November 1878.

Eli Fite. No. 170469. Postoffice Goodlettsville. Received an injury to his abdomen in service. He was placed on the pension rolls, June 1880.

Kesiah Work, No.30557. Postoffice, Madison. She was a widow of a Soldier of the War of 1812. Placed on pension rolls. Sept. 1880.

Sam'l M. Wilkerson, No.217103. Postoffice, Madison. He lost his first and second fingers in service. Placed on pension August 1882. He also contracted disease of heart and the lungs.

Edward M. Main, No.140527. Postoffice Madison. He received an injury of the wrist while in service. Pension allowed August 1876.

Ferrinia Hill Hamblin, No.14440. Postoffice was Madison. She was widow of a soldier of the War of 1812. Her application for pension was allowed January 1879.

James Lynam, No.149451. Postoffice, Nashville. He lost an eye and had head injuries during service. He was placed on pension rolls Nov. 1877.

Carrol Childes, No.54272. Postoffice address was Nashville. During service he lost a leg, therefore was placed on pension list Nov. 1866.

Harrison B. Carter, No.115951. Postoffice Nashville. Received injuries of leg, neck and head in service. Pensioned May 1872.

Houston Culp. No. 91687. Postoffice Nashville. During service lost a thumb. Placed on pension June 1868.

Herbert T. Judsen, No.3968. Postoffice Nashville. Inury te left arm while in service. Pensioned _____.

Jacob Hilderbrand (Hilderbrandt ?) No 119639. Post Office Nashville. Developed gangerene from an injury while in service. Pensioned Nov. 1872.

James B. Hogle. No.206838. Postoffice, Nashville. He received an injury to his abdomen; He also developed disease of the eye. Placed on pension April 1882.

Jonas Howard, No.87920. Postoffice was Nashville. Injury to left forearm. Placed on Pension 1867.

Joseph Hardin, No.74456. Postoffice Nashville. Injury to right leg in service. Pensioned November 1866.

Joseph Huttel, No.141735. Postoffice Nashville. Lost his right forearm in service. Pensioned October 1878.

Lorenzo G. Hogle. No.125,781. Postoffice Nashville. Injury to left side spurm and cord. Placed on pension, Feb. 1878. He also had other injuries.

Sam'l M. Holt, No.93555. Postoffice Nashville. Inury to the right leg in service. Pensioned October 1868.

Josiah Stull, No.8813. Postoffice Nashville. Injury to his left hand while in service. Pensioned January 1858.

Henry Bridges, No.3948. Postoffice Nashville. He was a soldier of the War of 1812. Pensioned Sept. 1871.

Allon T. Edmunds, No.4120. Postoffice. Nashville. Soldier in the War of 1812. Pensioned Sept. 1871.

Francis Brimley Fogg, No. 21371. Postoffice Nashville. Widow of a soldier of the War of 1812. Placed on pension list April 1874.

James Goodner, No.5938. Postoffice. Nashville. Soldier of the War of 1812. Placed on Pension November 1872.

Thomas Gale, No. 2139. Postoffice Nashville. He was a soldier in the War of 1812. Placed on pension October 1873.

Henry Holt, Sr., No. 2535. Postoffice Nashville. Soldier of the War of 1812. Placed on pension August 1871.

Jno. Moore, No.5327. Postoffice Nashville. He was a Soldier of the War of 1812. Placed on pension rolls. September 1873.

Nathaniel W.Moore, No.1602. Postoffice Nashville.
Soldier in the War of 1812. Placed on pension July 1871.

Hughey McAddams, No.17912. Postoffice Nashville.
Soldier of the War of 1812. Placed on pension July 1872.

Rachel Kellogg. No.10652. Postoffice, Nashville.
Widow of War of 1812 soldier. Placed on pension Nov. 1878

Martha L.Kitkpatrick, No.26597. Postoffice Nashville.
She was a widow of a soldier of the War of 1812. She was
allowed pension August 1879.

Lucy Michie, No.5917. Postoffice Nashville. She was
a widow of a Soldier of the War of 1812. Her pension was
allowed January 1874.

Eberline Moses, No.24655. Postoffice Nashville, She
was a widow of a Soldier of the War of 1812. Allowed pension
June 1879.

Harry M. McEwen, No.15555. Postoffice Nashville.
She was a widow of a soldier of the War of 1812 and was
allowed pension January 1879.

Eliz. A. Matthias, No.20696. Postoffice Nashville.
Her husband was a soldier of the War of 1812. She was placed
on pension March 1879.

America A. Miller. No.21333. Postoffice Nashville.
She was widow of a soldier of the War of 1812. Placed on
pension March 1879.

Nelley Norman, No.150839. Postoffice Nashville.
She was a widow. Pensioned May 1871.

Martha Moody, No. 191609. Postoffice. Nashville.
She was a widow, and placed on pension March 1881.

Seely Mills, No. 194460. Postoffice Nashville.
Was a widow. Placed on pension February 1882.

Ann Moore, No. 84652. Postoffice Nashville. Was
a widow. Placed on pension September 1866.

Charity Malone, No.76859. Postoffice Nashville.
She was a widow and was allowed pension June 1866.

Kate McSloane, No. 168105. Postoffice Nashville.
Was a widow and allowed pension Feby 1868.

Lucinda McKennedy, No.110612. Postoffice Nashville.
Was a widow. Placed on pension March 1868.

William Moore, No.108755. Postoffice Nashville.
Was a child. He was allowed a pension April 1878. **His
father was** evidently deceased.

Lucin Laughlinhouse, No.146009. Post **Office was
Nashville.** She was a widow. Allowed Pension **November 1870.**

Sally Lanier, No.132801. Postoffice Nashville.
Was a widow. Placed on pension August 1869.

Catherine O'Donohue, No.170178. Postoffice Nashville.
She was a widow and had a child. Placed on pension **July 1875.**

Eliza Ford, No.140003. **Postoffice was Nashville. She
was** a widow and was placed on pension 1870.

Silvey **Freeman, No.151809. Postoffice Nashville.
She was** a widow. Allowed pension July 1871.

Frances Ford, No.185293 **Postoffice Nashville. She
was** a widow and had a child. Placed on pension August 1879.

Melissa Abernathy. No. 91003. **Postoffice Nashville.**
She was a widow. Placed on pension **March 1867.**

**Fannie A.E. Johnson No.175332. Postoffice Nashville.
She was** a widow and was placed on pension October 1876.

Henrietta Joyce, No. 132930. Postoffice Nashville.
She was a widow and was placed on pension August 1869.

Elizabeth Branam, No. 16532. Postoffice Nashville.
Widow of War 1812 soldier. Allowed pension January 1879.

Martha M. Blumkall, No. 18450. Post **Office Nashville.
Widow** of War of 1812 Soldier. Placed on pension **February
1879.**

Rebecca Reese, No.6590. Post Office.Nashville. Tenn.
Widow of War of 1812 Soldier. Placed on pension May 1875.

Eliz P. Sigler, (Siglar), No. 23764. Postoffice
Nashville. Widow of War of 1812 soldier. Placed on pension
roll May 1879.

Eliza M. Stewart, No. 26581. Post Office Nashville.
She was a widow of a soldier of the War of 1812. **Pensioned**
August 1879.

Massey Vaughn. Mo.9641. Postoffice,Nashville. Tenn.
Was in service during the War of 1812. Placed on pension **Oct.**
1878.

Ann H Wray, No. 15057. Post Office Nashville. She
was widow of a soldier of the War of 1812. She was placed on
pension January 1879.

Martha Zachary, No.9920. Post Office Nashville. She
was the widow of a soldier of the War of 1812. She was placed
on pension October 1878.

Elizabeth Havely, No.16824. Postoffice, Nashville.
She was the widow of a soldier of the War of 1812. She was
allowed pension February 1879.

Edith Hobson, No.19001. Postoffice Nashville. Her
husband was a soldier in the War of 1812. Her pension began
February 1879.

Sarah Huggins, No.6632. Postoffice Nashville, Tenn.
Her husband was a soldier in the War of 1812 and she began
to draw pension July 1875.

Elizabeth W. Harding. No.31131. Postoffice Nashville.
She was widow of a soldier of the War of 1812 and was allowed
pension January 1881.

Esther Red, No.83130. Postoffice Nashville, widow and
child or children of a man who had been in service. Pensioned
January 1867.

Rhoda Drake, No.14208. Postoffice Nashville. Widow of
the War of 1812, placed on pension January 1879.

Frances A.Dix, No. 21516. Postoffice, Nashville,
widow of the war of 1812. pensioned March 1879.

Sarah Elrod, No.3046. Postoffice, Nashville. She was
the widow of a Soldier of the War of 1812 and was placed on
pension June 1872.

Sarah D. Eaton, No.16903. Postoffice Nashville. Was
the widow of a soldier of the War of 1812 and was allowed a
pension February 1879.

Lucinda Garner, No. 27182. Postoffice Nashville.
She was widow of a soldier in the War of 1812 and was allowed
to be placed on the pension rolls September 1879.

Mary Ann Gray, No.32223. Postoffice Nashville. She
was placed on the pension rolls February 1882.

Elizabeth D. Gilbert, No.21489. Postoffice Nashville.
She was a widow and placed on the rolls for pension in March
1879.

Sarah Anderson, No. 171195. Postoffice Nashville.
A widow. placed on the pension rolls 1875.

Caroline Beasley, No. 66004. Postoffice Nashville.
A widow. placed on pension March 1866.

Louisa Britton, No.78749. Postoffice Nashville.
Placed on pension August 1871. She was a widow.

Margaret L. Bearden, No.149872. Postoffice.Nashville.
She was the mother of a soldier and was placed on the pension
list April 1871.

Charles Luck, No.60795. Postoffice Nashville. Was
injured the left forearm in service. Placed on pension
March 1866.

Winifred S.Miller, No.60547. Postoffice Nashville.
Lost his left leg in service. Placed on pension March 1866.

William H.Montgomery, No. 76949. Postoffice Nashville.
Injured right leg in service. He was placed on pension
February 1867.

Tobias C. Miller, No.38787. Postoffice Nashville.
Injured right leg and foot in service.He was placed on
pension March 1865.

Moses McKnight. No. 84016. Postoffice Nashville.
Injury to left knww. He was placed on pension August 1867.

Joseph F. McFarling, No.63562. Postoffice Nashville.
Injured in right thigh during service and placed on pension
May 1866.

Jno. Mullen. No.210302, Postoffice Nashville. Was
wounded in the left arm in service. Allowed pension June
1882.

Hays Moore, No. 135922. Postoffice Nashville. He
received an injury in the right shoulder and in this breast
in service. Placed on pension Sept. 1875.

Francis Gillis. No. 176145. Postoffice Nashville.
Rheumatism and injury in left thigh in service. Pensioned
October 1880.

Francis M.Hamilton. No.215388. Postoffice Nashville.
wounded in right knee during service and placed on pension
July 1882.

Alfred Harris, No.179211. Postoffice Nashville.
During service received an injury in left leg. Pensioned Nov.
1880.

Sarah Childress Pplk, No.195476. Postoffice Nashville.
Widow. Placed on pension April 1882. (NOTE- This is the widow
of President James Knox Polk---ERW).

Regane Phips, No.1874. Postoffice Nashville. Widow.
Allowed pension September 1869.

Jane Pickett, No. 139102. Postoffice Nashville.
Mother of a deceased soldier. Placed on pension January 1871.

Priscilla Polk. No.124268. Postoffice Nashville. Widow.
Pensioned Feby 1869.

Sophia House, No. 73344. Postoffice Nashville. Widow.
Placed on pension rolls October 1867.

Fannie Helmes (Holmes?), No. 134342. Postoffice
Nashville. She was a widow. Allowed pension January 1870.

Emma Hogg. No.171435. Postoffice Nashville. A widow.
Allowed pension December 1875.

Sarah Hilton, No.195607. Postoffice Nashville. Mother
of a deceased soldier. Placed on pension May 1882.

Alfred Hamilton, No, 190722. Postoffice Nashville.
He was a child of a deceased soldier and was placed on the
pension rolls January 1881.

Comfort E. Harper, No. 187779. Postoffice Nashville.
She was the mother of a deceased soldier. She was placed on
the pension roll. April 1880.

Lydia Hunter, No. 185626. Postoffice Nashville.
Mother of a deceased soldier. Placed on pension September 1879.

Nancy Tate, No.1576. Postoffice Nashville. She was
a widow and placed on the pension rolls May 1874.

Frank Turner, No. 170616. Postoffice Nashville.
A child of a deceased soldier. Placed on pension Sept. 1875.

Milla Vassell. No.143006. Postoffice Nashville. A widow
and placed on pension June 1870.

Rachel Vickery, No.128553. Postoffice Nashville.
The mother of a deceased service man. Allowed pension March
1869.

Rebecca Robinson, No. 130311. Postoffice Nashville.
She was a widow and allowed pension December 1880.

Pauline Rabb (Robb?), No.152748. Postoffice Nashville.
A widow. Placed on pension August 1871.

Elizabeth Smith, No.110619. Postoffice Nashville.
Was the mother of a deceased service man. Allowed pension
March 1868.

Helena Schaefer, No.156959. Postoffice Nashville.
She was a widow and allowed pension March 1872.

Elmira Smith, No. 114783. Postoffice Nashville,
She was a widow and was granted a pension July 1870.

James J. Barnard, No 168711. Postoffice Nashville.
He was injured in service in the right arm. He was allowed
a pension May 1880.

Jno. Been. No.74364. Postoffice Nashville. He
lost his left arm above the elbow in service of his country.
He was pensioned October 1874

Sarah Winchester, No.189731. Postoffice Nashville.
She was the mother of a deceased service man. She was allowed
a pension September 1880.

Mary Wallace. No. 83541. Postoffice Nashville. Was
a widow and placed on the pension rolls Dec. 1868.

Mary E. Weidenbacker, No.173703. Postoffice Nashville.
She was a widow with children and was placed on pension
June 1876.

Maria Washington, No. 128876. Postoffice Nashville.
She was a widow of a service man and placed on pension Nov.
1869.

Emily Walker, No.89794. Postoffice Nashville. She was
the mother of a service man who was deceased and she was
granted a pension February 1867.

Cynthia Williamson. No. 3727. Postoffice Nashville.
She was a widow and received a pension.

Sarah Cowham (Cowhom) No.160547. Postoffice Nashville.
She was a widow and placed on pension December 1872.

Martha Combs. No. 150825. Postoffice. Was a widow and
granted pension May 1871.

Margaret Coolican, No. 89896. Postoffice Nashville.
Was a widow and placed on pension February 1864.

Fannie Cookerel, No.130310.Postoffice Nashville.
She was a widow and allowed pension June 1866.

Lucy Chambers, No.105196. Postoffice Nashville. She
was a widow and allowed to go on the pension rools, December
1861.

Rebecca Gathen, No.78541. Postoffice Nashville. She
was a widow and allowed to go on pension July 1867.

Mary Grundy, No.150200. Postoffice Nashville. She
was a widow and placed on pension May 1879.

Bridget M. Guerin. No.86101. Postoffice Nashville.
She was a widow and placed on pension October 1877.

Anna Gravey, No.125935. Postoffice Nashville. She
was placed on pension March 1869.

Laura Gant. No.189150. Postoffice, Nashville. Was the
mother of a deceased service man. Her pension began July
1880.

Mahalay Gardner, No. 193998. Postoffice Nashville.
She was a widow and allowed pension January 1882.

Eveline Gresham. No. 186807. Postoffice Nashville.
She was a widow with child or children and was granted a
pension January 1880.

Patrick Gleason, No. 140397. Postoffice Nashville.
He received an injury in the right hip during service.
Placed on pension August 1876.

Alexander Harley, No. 52362. Postoffice Nashville.
Wounded in left arm during his service. Pensioned Nov. 1865.

Gottfried Lammeister, 120523. Postoffice Nashville.
Wounded in the right leg during service. Pensioned December
1872.

George F. Sweeney, No. 2222. Postoffice Nashville.
He served in the Navy. Took Chronic dynesentary   He was
pensioned March 1876.

Henry Gerding, No.146981. Postoffice Nashville.
He was wounded in the abdomen. Placed on pension July 1877.

Wealthy Vigus, No.20009. Postoffice Nashville.
She was the widow of an 1812 Soldier and was placed on pension
March 1879.

Gregory C. McDermot. No.148655. Postoffice Nashville.
He was wounded in the left thigh during term of service.
Placed on pension October 1882.

Wm.L. Shelby, No.33378. Postoffice Nashville.Injured
in the left breast and in the spine. Pensioned October 1864

Conrad Nass, No.207898. Postoffice Nashville. Dis-
abled due to service injury. Pensioned May 1882.

Jno. Smith, No. 198648. Postoffice Nashville.
Deafness and other injury during service. Pensioned Dec. 1881.

Mary B. Robertson . No. ____? Postoffice Nashville.
Her husband served in the Navy. She was a widow and was pensioned August 1868.

James Pickerl, No.51330. Postoffice Nashville. He
received a wound in the left shoulder while in service.
Was placed on pension October 1865.

Mathew Brisbo. No.31869. Postoffice Nashville. While
in service received a wound in the left arm, and was pensioned August 1861.

Geo.W. Wilson. No. 131396. Postoffice Nashville. He
was in service when he was wounded in the left knee joint.
Pensioned January 1875.

Chas. A. Reins, No.139848. Postoffice Nashville.
While in service lost two fingers on both hands. Pensioned
July 1876.

Chas.F. Armsbee, No.63535. Postoffice Nashville.
Received a wound in the left shoulder during term of service.
Was placed on pension May 1866.

Geo. D. Critchett, No.18383. Postoffice Nashville. He
was wounded in the right hand while in service. Allowed pension
October 1863.

Jno.Malloy, No.8593. Postofficce Nashville. While in
service received a wound in the left arm, for which he was
placed on service November 1856.

Alfred Newsom. No.97229. Postoffice Nashville. While
in service contracted "phthisis pulmondis". Pensioned
March 1875.

Alexander Bell. No. 163527. Postoffice Nashville.
While in service received injury in the abdomen. Placed on
pension roll. November 1879.

Henry Trauernicht. No.19000. Postoffice Nashville.
While serving a term in the service loss the left leg. Was
allowed pension November 1863.

66.

Jno.W. Austin, No.167672. Postoffice Nashville. While in service was wounded in the face and was placed on pension April 1880.

Heaekiah Avery, No 147896. Postoffice Nashville. During the time he was in service he was wounded in the right thigh. Allowed pension August 1877.

Charles Allen, No.127138. Postoffice.Nashville. While in service was wounded in the left leg and foot. He was placed on pension March 1874.

George Childers. No.218578. Postoffice Nashville. Was injured in the abdomen while he was in service. Pensioned Sept. 1882.

Wm. Chineult, No.140659. Postoffice Nashville. While in service was wounded in the left leg. Pensioned Aug.1876.

Patrick J.Cruise. No.144743. Postoffice Nashville. While in service received a fracture of the right leg for which he was pensioned October 1876.

Ellen Crawford, No. 22816. Postoffice Nashville. She was the widow of a soldier of the War of 1812. and was placed on the pension rolls April 1879.

Sarah Cunningham, No.5487. Postoffice Nashville. Placed on pension July 1873.

Elizabeth D. Cheatham, No.21292. Postoffice Nashville. Placed on pension March 1879.

Samuel Watkins, No.2427. Postoffice Nashville. He was a soldier in the War of 1812 and was placed on pension Aug. 1871.

Robert Endaley, No.59387. Postoffice Nashville. While in service he was wounded in the right forearm and in the breast. March 1866 was placed on pension,

Andrew Ewing, No.163907. Postoffice Nashville. Had "paranchylosis of left ankle" Placed on pension December 1879.

Adolph Esslinger, No.164952. Postoffice Nashville. While in service was wounded in the back. Placed on pension February 1880.

Abraham L. Earnheart, No.169300. Postoffice Nashville. Wounded in the right side. Placed on pension June 1880.

Wm.D.Dorris, No.6440. Postoffice Nashville. Developed Chronie rhenumatism. Placed on pension April 1867

Edward Dohoney, No.96472. Postoffice Nashville.
While in service was wounded in the left hand and arm.Lost
sight of one eye and weakness of the right eye. Pensioned
April 1862.

Chas. Davis. No. 3158. Postoffise Nashville. Pensioned
November 1846.

Wm.J.Nees. No.74973. Postoffice Nashville. Wound in
the forearm. Pensioned December 1866.

Wesley Baker, No.137691. Postoffice Nashville. Wound
in the right arm. Pensioned February 1876.

Thomas Burrowes. No.128187. Postoffice Nashville.
Disease of the lung contracted in service and pensioned   in
May 1874.

Sam'l J.Book. No.14331. Postoffice Nashville. During
service was wounded in the shoulder and back. Pensioned July
1863.

Michael Brannon, No.179634. Postoffice Nashville.
During service injured in abdomen. Pensioned December 1880.

Wm.Tucker, No.146851. Postoffice Nashville. Contracted
rheumatism in service. Pensioned. July 1877.

Jno.Beach (alias Jno.Whitsett). No.220664. Postoffice
Nashville. Wounded in the right leg. Pensioned November
1882.

Jno.Rathrop No.151425. Postoffice Nashville. Wound
in the leg. pensioned November 1878.

Max Rosenheim. No.37389. Postoffice Nashville. Lost
his arm in service. Pensioned January 1865.

David Redd. No.136519. Postoffice. Nashville. After
serving developed sore eyes and was pensioned November 1875.

Calvin S.Roberts, No.93376. Postoffice, Nashville.
Wounded in left foot in service. Pensioned October 1868.

Silas Smith, No. 222659. Postoffice Nashville.
Wounded in right arm. Pensioned December 1882.

Thomas Smith, No.136854. Postoffice Nashville.
Wounded in right hand. Amputated two fingers. Pensioned Nov.
1875.

James Scarbrough, No.125319. Postoffice Nashville.
Wounded in left arm. Pensioned. 1873

Lucius Sea, No.150383. Postoffice Nashville. Wounded
in left hand. Pensioned January 1878.

Abraham Sanders, No. 218657. Postoffice Nashville.
Wounded in right foot. Pensioned in October 1882.

Michael Walsh. No. 96858. Postoffice Nashville.
Contracted a disease in service. Pensioned February 1871

Madison White, No. 91759. Postoffice Nashville.
Received wound in right groin. Pensioned June 1868.

Jno.Williams. No.95341. Postoffice Nashville.
During service contracted chromic bronchitis and disease of
the legs. Placed on pension February 1869.

James Williamson. No.3240. Postoffice Nashville.
Lost his right arm above the elbow in service. Pensioned.
_____

James Williamson, No. 144469. Postoffice Nashville.
Injury to abdomen while in service. Pensioned April 1877.

Geo.L. Watson. No. 162711. Postoffice Nashville.
Wounded in the abdomen during service. Pensioned. October
1879.

Daniel Williams, No. 94084. Postoffice Nashville.
Injury to right foot during service. Pensioned. December 1868.

Chas. B. Wheelock. No. 49651. Postoffice Nashville.
Wounded in left side while in service. Pensioned. Sept.1865.

Michael Philips.No.179340. Postoffice Nashville,
Contracted disease of the hip and heart (?) while in
service. Pensioned December 1880.

Jno.Bentley. No.26376. Postoffice Nashville.
Wounded in the right foot during service. Pensioned April 1864.

Matilda Bass, No.95389. Postoffice Nashville. Widow.
Pensioned June 1867.

Rachel Bayne or Baines, No.177424. Postoffice Nashville. Was a widow. pensioned May 1877.

Nancy E. Blankenship. No.165774. Postoffice Nashville.
She was a widow. Pensioned July 1874.

Lucinda Raines, No. 28264, Postoffice Nashville.
She was the widow of a soldier of the War of 1812. She
was allowed pension December 1879.

Esther Waggoner, No. 23966. Postoffice, Rosedale.
She was a widow of a soldier of the War of 1812 and was
placed on pension May 1879.

Emily Hamilton, No.19369. Postoffice Stewart's
Ferry. She was a widow of a Soldier of the War of 1812
and was allowed pension March 1879.

Eliza A.Newland, No. 32464. Postoffice, White's
Creek. She was the widow of a soldier of the war of 1812
and was allowed pension June 1882.

INDEX......

78

Lightfoot, 17
Liles (Lile), 27, 37, 44
Linley, 21
Linear (Lenear) 29,30.
Linn, 33
Linton, 17, 26
Lins, 31
Lintz, 24
Lipscomb, 53
Little, 26
Livingston, 27
Locke, (Look), 22, 37
Lockhart, 14.
Loftin, 16
Logan, 7
Loggans, 12
Long, 12, 35, 42
Looney, 4, 7
Louge, 34, 35
Love. 12, 19, 30
Lovell (Lovel) 18, 33
Lowrt, 33
Lowry, 28
Loyd, 16
Lucas, 6,8,9,12, 22, 30
Luck, 61
Lugert, 28
Lumsden 9
Lusk, 28
Luthert, 31
Lynam, 56
Lynch, 17, 18
Lyles, 12
Lynn, 6, 12
Lytle, 23, 37

McAdams, 34, 40,42
McAddams, 58
MacAdoe, 8
McAllister (McAlister) 12,
    22.
McAntosh, 12
McBeam, 25
McBean, 36
McBride, 19, 20
McCaffrey, 25
McCain, 12, 14
McCame, 15
McCampbell. 17
McCann, 48
McCarnahan 24

McCarty 12
McCaslin. 22, 54
McClelland (McClellan) 17, 46
McCombs, 32
McCormack, 31, 33, 34, 35, 40
McCay, 25
McCrabb 47
McCrory, 14, 30
McCullom (McCollum), 16, 26
McCutchen, 13, 17, 30, 42, 53
McDaniel, 19, 22, 26, 37, 33,
McDermot, 64
McElwain, 40
McElwand, 37
McEwen, 30, 58
McEwing, 38
McFadden 13
McFaddin 14
McFarland, 12,14, 23
McFarlin. 13
McFarling, 61.
McFerrin 19
McGaugh, 16
McGaughey 27
McGavock, 13, 23, 25
McGough, 12
McGowan, 12
McGregor, 28
McHall 20
McIntosh, 23
McKay, 35
Mckennedy, 58
McKinney 14
McKnight, 61
McLain, 50
McLamore, 23
McLand, 34
McLane, 13
McLaughlin 32
McLoan, 17
McLin, 26
McLindon 32
McLovell, 18
M'Mahan, 50
McMurray 6
McMurry, 19, 43
McMurtry 9
McNairy, 13, 23, 36, 54
McNeal, 29
McNeese, 18, 19
McNight 12
McQuarry 16
McQueery 18

Poore, 50
Pope, 6
Porter, 4, 9, 15, 23, 24, 36, 45, 46.
Porterfield, 21
Powell, 27, 34, 55.
Power, 6
Prater, 8
Pratt 8
Price, 23
Pride, 35
Priest 24
Priestly, 20, 37
Prince, 13, 25
Pritchett, 15, 23, 26
Probart, 24
Prochman 13
Pryor, 26, 36
Puckett, 22
Pulley, 36
Pullin, 19
Purnell, 4

Qnaw, 55
Quarles, 19,
Questenberry 36
Quigley, 6, 9

Rabb (Robb), 62
Ragan, 34
Ragland, 17
Raines (Rains), 17, 21, 69
Ralph, 15
Paslton, 13, 22
Ramsey, 8, 13, 17, 18, 24
Randal. 34
Randolph 30
Raner, 33
Rape, 37
Rasberry, 18, 20
Raser (Rasor), 29, 33
Ratfelt, 6
Rathrop, 67
Raworth, 23
Ray, 6,8,13,36 , 21
Raymond, 15.
Read (Reed), 6, 13,24,22,33.
Reading, 30
Reaves (Rieves) 16,17,27, 37.

Reckner, 13
Reding, 55
Redd (Red) 60, 67
Reddin, 31
Reeder, 35
Reese, 52, 59
Reeves, 50
Reins, 65
Renfree 4
Renfrew 9
Rentfro, 24
Rice, 23, 29, 35.
Richard, 24
Richardson, 18, 23, 25, 26, 36, 37, 43
Hickey 29
Ridge, 33
Ridley, 21
Riley, 18
Ripsumer 27
Ritchey 33
Roach, 14, 26
Roads, 26
Roan, 25, 36
Robeson, 7
Roberts, 13, 19, 21, 20, 47, 67, 50.
Robertson, 6,8, 7,13, 17, 23, 24, 27, 36, 48, 50 ,65
Robinson, 15, 62
Rogan, 4, 43
Rogers (Roger), 36, 33, 31, 43, 45, 52.
Roland, 28
Roper, 24
Rosenheim, 67
Ross, 13, 28
Rounsevall, 8,10,13
Rounsifer, 4
Rowe, 45
Rower, 35
Rucker, 15, 28
Ruddle, 7
Ruland, 13
Rurff, 36
Rusk, 28
Russell, 6, 18
Rutherford, 25, 43, 50

Sadler, 37
Sage, 50

www.ingramcontent.com/pod-product-compliance
Lightning Source LLC
Chambersburg PA
CBHW070256290326
41930CB00041B/2592